# The English Project

# The English Project

Edited by Pat D'Arcy

# Stage Three **Bonds**

Ward Lock Educational

Designed by IKON
Set in Monophoto Garamond and printed by
BAS Printers Limited, Over Wallop, Hampshire

for Ward Lock Educational
116 Baker Street, London W1M 2BB
Made in Great Britain

# Contents

# Watching Song

**1**

Watch, I warn you,
By night and starlight,
You who are chosen to
Stand on the brick-built
Walls of Modena:
Wait for the dawn-hour.

**2**

Standing at arms and
Peering in darkness
Over the flatlands;
Pacing slowly
On open stretches
Of mortared levels or
Close in catwalks;
Pause and listen,
With lowered eyelid and
Heart under breastplate:
Question the silence.

3

– Nothing but frogs
That chatter in ditches,
And crying of nightbirds.
Yet we watch to
Outwit the sorrowful,
Shag-haired rabble of
Heathen raiders.

4

And so in our sentries
Bound and helmeted,
Over the city
We sing out watches,
Call on the Name and
Summon our safety –
Singing in antiphon,
Answer in unison,
'Lord God omnipotent,
Shield and companion:

5

'Saviour and King,
And crown of mankind;
You who were born for
Our peace, to stand over us,
Keep your hand over us.'

6

Then, as the song goes,
Hear it echoing
Round by the walls
Of the guarded city,
Floating by tenements,
Roofs and courtyards,
Domes of churches and
Empty markets –
Stirring and comforting
Drowsy families,
Strangers at inns and
Close-laid lovers:
The patient candle
Of cellared workmen
Yawning at benches:
Shuttered taverns,
And prayers in silence,
And lamps by altars
That live in darkness.

7

Then watch together, singing together
And stand as faithful,
Hearing it echo
Round the walls we
Keep in safety,
Until the first breath
Sent from the dawn-hour
Touches the night's face,
And the dawn brightens.

**F. T. Prince**

# Strange Meeting

As Hilliard stepped out of the stables, he heard the splashing sound of a horse beginning to urinate against the stone floor.

Ahead of him, the shadow of a man, standing at the top of the drive.

'Hilliard?'

Barton.

'I thought I'd walk with you for a bit, if that's all right.' His voice was friendly.

Hilliard had thought that what he wanted was to be alone, to go down between the fruit trees and into the dark lane and get his bearings. But now, with Barton standing in front of him, he realized that he did not, that he had had more than enough of walking by himself, of his own thoughts and memories and despair, had had too much solitariness, at Hawton.

He said, 'Yes, do.'

Barton fell into step with him on the rough farmyard path. Away to the west, a succession of green Verey flares lit up the sky, followed by the guns. Then it went black again, as they came down into the lane facing a belt of trees. Again, Hilliard heard the sound of water.

'If we go up here and turn off to the left we come into another orchard. It leads across to the church eventually. There's a bit of a stream.'

Hilliard nodded and they went that way. The air smelled damp, there might be some mist at dawn.

He thought, I should remember this, I should remember everything about it, for it will not last. At once, the atmosphere around him seemed too insubstantial to be remembered, it was nothing, was only a walk between trees and through long grass at night, there were the usual sounds and smells, the hidden movements of small creatures in the undergrowth. There was nothing in particular to remember. And everything.

'*We're for the front again next week, sir.*'

The men always heard rumours and the rumours spread and turned out to be the truth.

Their footsteps swished through the grass. They came nearer to the sound of water.

'I'm glad you've come,' Barton said easily.

They went as far as the edge of the stream and then sat down, leaning against some willows. Barton lit a cigarette and the sparks flickered upwards through the leaves of the tree. His eyes and the lower half of his face were in darkness, but the line of his nose, with its high, narrow bridge, gleamed bone-white. The tree trunks were like pewter.

Looking at him, Hilliard thought that Barton was handsome, and that he would have liked to introduce him to Beth. That thought had never occurred to him with any man before, probably because he had taken so few friends home. But he dismissed the idea almost at once, for Beth was too old, was twenty-four, was plain and about to marry the lawyer Henry Partington. Thinking of the new person she had become, he knew that she would not understand anything about Barton. He was not sure if he did so himself. But he wanted to understand. Beth might not.

'I didn't expect it to be like this,' Barton was saying. His knees were up to his chin, head forward as he looked at the water. 'I'd heard all the things you do hear about the war. I hadn't expected it to be such a pleasant life.'

'We are in rest camp, you know.'

You wait, he should be saying, you wait. But where was the point of that? Barton would find out, soon enough.

'All the same, it's a bit like being back at OTC. Rather boring. I thought at least we'd be under shell fire or sharing a room with some rats.'

'Is that what you were looking forward to?'

'Oh God, no!'

'Then why say it? And this won't last forever.'

'No. I didn't want to come out here at all, I was in a blue funk. I'd have done more or less anything . . . but I'm fit and of age, I couldn't slip through the net. So I suppose I'd better make the most of it.'

'Do you always tell people everything you're feeling?'

Barton looked round at him in surprise. 'Generally. If I want to. If they want to hear.' He paused and then laughed. 'Good Lord, we're not at school now, are we?'

Hilliard did not reply.

'Besides, it's the way we were brought up. To say things, tell people what you feel. I don't mean to force it on anyone. But not to bottle things up.'

'I see.'

'It's my father mainly. He's pretty busy so we might easily go through life seeing hardly anything of him. He makes a point of seeing each of us alone, for a while, every week, finding out what we're doing, asking if we've anything to tell him, you know? It's a bit like having an appointment in his surgery really!'

'He's a doctor?'

'Yes.'

'When you say "we . . ." '

'There are six of us. Three brothers older than me, two sisters, younger. We all came tumbling one after another though, so we seem much of an age. It's good that way, especially now. We've always been close, of course, but when you're small children you just take that for granted, don't you?'

Do you? Hilliard tried to decide. Yes, he had been close to Beth. But that had changed, now they were older, separated.

He said, 'I have one sister.'

'Younger?'

'No, she's twenty-four.'

'Is she married?'

'She – not yet.'

'Tell her to get a move on, then you can have all your nephews and nieces – you'll enjoy that.'

'Shall I?'

'Oh, of course. I do. I get on with my sisters best, I think. Both of them are married now.'

Barton slid down the tree-trunk into the grass, resting on his arm. 'No, I withdraw that, there's really no difference between any of us,

we all live out of one another's pockets. And the brothers-in-law now. They've just been absorbed into the family! I shan't like it being out here and not seeing any of them. We're all so split up now.'

'Haven't your brothers joined up?'

'One's got exemption because he has tuberculosis. Dick's in the RAMC but he's gone out to Egypt. My youngest brother's in prison.' He talked about them as though he had never in his life found any reason to keep things back. Hilliard was slightly embarrassed.

'He's a conchy. I nearly was, but then I realized it was nothing to do with conscience, it was just because I was frightened and wanted to get out of coming to France. Edward's different, he really means it. He put up a terrific fight, and he's having a rotten time, it isn't much fun for him. I'm better off than he is, at the moment.'

What he felt most of all was envy of Barton. He tried to picture what it would be like to have a family, to whom you were so close, about whom you could talk so lovingly, people you missed every day, and admitted to missing. What would it feel like? What kind of people were they, all these Bartons? What did they say and do together?

'I suppose you didn't much want to come back either, did you? Especially since you already know what it's like?'

'I don't . . .' But there seemed no way he could begin to explain, not without telling everything about himself. He had never done that.

Barton had moved forward and was leaning his arm down into the stream. 'This is pretty well dried up,' he said thoughtfully. 'I wonder how long since it rained?'

Something seemed to click inside Hilliard. It was all right. Barton was all right. He could talk, after all, could tell him anything.

'I didn't mind coming back,' he said, 'it was so bloody awful at home. I couldn't stick it. Not that I forgot what it had been like out here – I had nightmares about it. Nobody ever forgets. But I couldn't bear to stay on at home, to stay in England at all, it's . . . I can't explain. I wish I could tell you.'

'Tell me,' Barton said simply. He still lay on his stomach, hand dabbling gently in the water. His legs were very long, reaching back through the grass towards Hilliard.

He had been waiting for someone, just as Garrett had waited for him. Waiting for Barton. Though he had not known it. Long ago, he would have talked to Beth. Not now. There had never been anyone else close enough.

'Go on. Tell me.'

Hilliard did so. It was not difficult, after all.

**Susan Hill**

# Roman Wall Blues

Over the heather the wet wind blows,
I've lice in my tunic and a cold in my nose.

The rain comes pattering out of the sky,
I'm a Wall soldier, I don't know why.

The mist creeps over the hard grey stone,
My girl's in Tungria; I sleep alone.

Aulus goes hanging around her place,
I don't like his manners, I don't like his face.

Piso's a Christian, he worships a fish;
There'd be no kissing if he had his wish.

She gave me a ring but I diced it away;
I want my girl and I want my pay.

When I'm a veteran with only one eye
I shall do nothing but look at the sky.

**W. H. Auden**

# First Frost

A girl is freezing in a telephone booth,
huddled in her flimsy coat,
her face stained by tears
and smeared with lipstick.

She breathes on her thin little fingers.
Fingers like ice. Glass beads in her ears.

She has to beat her way back alone
down the icy street.

First frost. A beginning of losses.
The first frost of telephone phrases.

It is the start of winter glittering on her cheek,
the first frost of having been hurt.

**Andrei Voznesensky** *translated by Stanley Kunitz*


# Lizard

The lizard of love
Has fled my grasp once again
And left its tail between my fingers.
Just as well
I would have wanted to keep it for myself.

**Jacques Prévert**

# Wedding Wind

The wind blew all my wedding-day,
And my wedding-night was the night of the high wind;
And a stable door was banging, again and again,
That he must go and shut it, leaving me
Stupid in the candlelight, hearing rain,
Seeing my face in the twisted candlestick,
Yet seeing nothing. When he came back
He said the horses were restless, and I was sad
That any man or beast that night should lack
The happiness I had.

Now in the day
All's ravelled under the sun by the wind's blowing.
He has gone to look at the floods, and I
Carry a chipped pail to the chicken-run,
Set it down, and stare. All is the wind
Hunting through clouds and forests, thrashing
My apron and the hanging cloths on the line.
Can it be borne, this bodying-forth by wind
Of joy my actions turn on, like a thread
Carrying beads? Shall I be let to sleep
Now this perpetual morning shares my bed?
Can even death dry up
These new delighted lakes, conclude
Our kneeling as cattle by all-generous waters?

**Philip Larkin**

# Hymeneal

Susan Edden, just married, comes to the farm in 1921. Up the hill, but down in status, according to her mother, the doctor's wife. She has spent her life on the edge of, but never in farms. She comes up with Jesse ('Jesse,' her mother says, 'sounds like a girl. Is that a name for a man?') in the cart, not her father's car. Starting, she says, with a crispness that comes naturally to her, as she means to go on. But really because she fancies it.

Even outside the church, the two families keep to themselves. Eddens stiff and sweating in tight best suits; Aitkens moving easily in their clothes, capturing the vicar. Kisses, handkerchiefs, tears, some Aitken confetti, then suddenly, miraculously, from the Edden side great boughs and branches of orange blossom and lilac, spread at their feet, piled in the cart. Jesse swearing and blinking behind flowers. Joe, father Edden, missing, then up the road comes a flowering bush, swaying, almost a tree, all white. It seems a long time coming. The light shakes. Then, shedding some flowers, it is tumbled across their laps into the cart. And Joe colours and winks, first one eye, then the other, and just as embarrassing remarks and damp farewells seem inevitable, he thumps the mare, like a barmaid, on the backside, and she shivers, farts and leads off.

Someone has stuck cow-parsley in the mare's harness and hung two little bells on the reins. The white dusty blooms tickle her ears. It is a light cart. She trots and the bells ring. Between the village and the bare hill there is a natural avenue of bushes and trees. They move under white hawthorn, between high green, on their throne of boughs. Susan leans against her husband's shoulder. He puts an arm round her, leaving one hand for the reins.

'It was a lovely idea,' she says, and when he seems not to understand: 'the flowers.' Inside her head her voice sounds artificial, patronizing. She would like to swallow her words, but no harm is done. He seems wrapped in some dream of his own. He is a small, brown, slim man, his only weakness, it appears to her, a shyness at having snatched her from the arms of suitable young men. She must reassure him. She blesses, for once, her intelligence, which will find a way to convince him of her love, his own worth.

He grunts: 'They'll want a do.'

'Yes,' she says, 'of course. They'll expect it. For them.'

'And you. It would be right.'

'Oh, me. I don't care about things like that.'

'You're a funny one.' For the first time since they were married, half an hour ago, he really looks at her, puzzled and loving. 'You know what you're in for? What you've lost?' He touches her cheek.

She laughs, clear-throated, easy. So that's what bothers him.

'If you knew . . . how boring those people are. What you've saved me from.'

'Perhaps.'

'Hurry,' she says, 'hurry. I want to begin.' They are out of the avenue and there is the hill and the house. She wants to throw open the windows, bring in flowers. The horse stops trotting and plods. 'Make her go fast.' She is excited and wants to tease him. 'Or don't you whip mares?'

'Oh yes,' he says. 'They're all the same, beasts.'

She likes to see him so sure with the reins. Something her father could not do. She congratulates herself on her instinct in choosing this man. She wishes only that she could spark off the same excitement in him. He kisses her softly on the cheek and touches the mare with the whip. They trot up the hill, shedding flowers.

The yard is smaller than she remembers, the ugly black barn bigger.

A skinny dog runs out and barks at them. He swears gently and it retreats, after a moment's doubt, wagging and cursing, backing to its place under the barn.

'No, he says, 'the front door.'

They go through the side gate, stiff, never used, to the front of the house. He has to kick the hinge. Between the house and the hedge there is half an acre of freshly turned earth. He is proud of this and shy. She knows that she must look pleased, though it's hard to imagine, at this moment, what she might do with it. He points to the boundaries. He has spent every evening in the last month, from nine to eleven, digging.

'There! That's yours. Your garden.' Anxious: 'You like flowers? You said?'

'Yes,' she says, and kisses him. 'Thank you. I love it.' Love, lovely, seem the only words she can say today. They don't mean much. They have been rubbed flat of meaning. But he doesn't notice. He uses words as the nearest tools that come to hand, rough and ready. Some fresher for his simplicity. She tells herself, I must go carefully; show him but not spoil him. She talks about roses and they go in.

She serves the cold chicken, puts away clothes and arranges her books. She can see how she might make this house her own, in time, with tact. Her mother caught her packing the books and said: 'You'll have no time for them.' 'Then I'll make time.'

'Your reading,' he murmurs, touching their spines as if they held secrets. 'I can hardly read more than my name.'

'I'll teach you if you like.'

'If there's time. Yes. I'd like that.' He looks at her in wonder. 'You're a queen, you know.'

She smiles. She is entirely happy and convinced of the rightness of her choice. 'But you too. You can do things I know nothing about. I'll be a fool, I know, on a farm. You'll have to show me.'

'You'll learn.'

After they have drunk tea (she would have preferred coffee but the tea, after all, tastes right) they go up. There is no electricity here, or gas. She is enchanted by the low roofed room and the oil lamps. She turns them down and waits in the dark. She thinks he will be shy. He smells of soap.

'You've shaved.'

'Yes.'

'Kiss me.'

They have kissed often. This is familiar. She likes it, would like to prolong it. She feels very powerful, able to please him.

'Don't stop.' He pauses, propped above her on one elbow. His voice is baffled, almost resentful.

'Why did you marry me?'

She refuses to take him seriously. 'Now . . . let me see.'

'Not my money or my looks.' He is still solemn, quite stern. 'Nor my reading. Was it a fancy?'

'Jesse! What do you think I am?'

'I think you're a clever young woman, who, if choice were hers, would maybe never marry. Not as clever as you think. And you'd not be as content alone as you'll imagine, in bad times.'

She is touched by his seriousness. 'We'll have no bad times. I know it. Or none we can't overcome.'

He seems not to have heard her.

'And you wanted to do something with yourself. You've got pride in yourself. But you didn't know what. Just that it had to be something the others don't do. You might have gone to one of those universities, been a teacher. But you fancied me.'

'That's a terrible thing to say!' She is near to tears. They are whispering as if in Church. She had thought she held him, quiet and small, in the palm of her hand.

'No. For most that's what it comes down to, fancies. All I say is, Susan, don't build on me, not too much. That is, you can count on me always, I hope. But don't think I can be owt but myself.'

'I don't understand!'

'It doesn't matter. It was best said now.' He smiles and pulls her hands away from her eyes. Then he begins to laugh and romp like a young dog. He fools about, and kisses and tries to be gentle, but it still hurts, more than she could have believed possible. At once, he falls asleep. She lies awake, hurt and bewildered. He takes her once more in the night, without even opening his eyes. This time it is better. But her wedding night is not at all what she expected.

The next three days – a long weekend – are good. The farm is still small. It will grow in the next forty years, but now it is possible for Jesse to take a short holiday. Through the four-day honeymoon an Edden cousin and another man keep things going but avoid the house, averting their eyes as they follow their sloped shadows across the yard when, in the early morning, woken by unfamiliar farm noises, Susan appears at the window.

'There's Tam. I think I've shocked him.'

He plunges his head in the bowl, pokes soap out of his ears.

'Not Tam. He thinks you're Queen of England.'

'And you?'

'I'll show you what I think. Give me that towel.'

'I might and I might not.'

He lunges after her, blind with soap, groping. 'You're a skinny cat.'

She sidesteps. Wherever she goes, he follows, but slow, threatening and swearing, roaring. It's like having a blind bull on a chain. They are behaving like children. This is the best time they will have.

'Give.'

'Say I'm the Queen of England.'

'I'm boggered if I will.'

He pins her down at last and wipes his eyes on the sheet. These are silly, private jokes. Instinctively, from a sensibility with which she does not credit him, he gives her all the nonsense she wants, but does not know she wants. She may deny later, even to herself, that she has ever been so frivolous. She has gone into this marriage, she likes to think, with her eyes open, determined that it shall be good and lasting: she sees them as reasonable friends, teaching each other. He will learn to read, to listen to music (for which she feels he has a natural, if untutored ear); she to be a farmer's wife. Concerning the second project she is vague but optimistic. She has always been competent. As for his education, that will be a matter of tact and patience and love. Their marriage will be all the richer – out of the ordinary – for these mutual benefits. She brings a great if invisible dowry and has a brain clear enough and a temperament cool enough ('Susan is such a *sensible* girl') to bestow it without offence or patronage. This is how her mind runs. She prizes her mind more than her looks. On one subject she might admit she is a romantic – common sense.

In these four days – after that first, odd night – her sensible resolutions are blurred by happiness. She notices, on the fourth day, that he is restless. His hands on the fine tablecloth (her mother's present) look foolish and empty. He wants to get back to work.

'You're worried about the farm?'

'The lambing's started. Tam's no shepherd. We can't afford to lose them.'

'Shall we go and see?' She has noticed the pen in the sloping field behind the house, up in the corner, where the hedge makes a windbreak.

'You wouldn't mind?'

'I'd like to.'

'You're a good girl.'

'No. I'm just your wife. Besides –' she adds, with something of her natural airs – 'I've never seen an animal born.'

'It might be best if you stayed.'

'No. I want to come. If I won't be in the way?'

'You' he says, and touches her cheek, 'you.'

They walk up the hill hand in hand. Up here there is a wind and the stars seem to be running, racing, falling. The couple pause for breath and look up:

'It's fine,' he says.

'Yes. It's lovely. You know them?'

'No. Only the Plough.' He jabs his thumb where the stars seem windiest. 'And the Milky Way. Tam knows them. He's learned them from fishing.' She knows what he means but likes to imagine Tam, sturdier and blacker than his cousin, monosyllabic, drawing in his trawling net great shoals of stars. She doesn't mention this. It sounds like the fancy of a silly girl. She frowns, as if dazzled, and says, offhand:

'It's strange to think some of them are dead. We're seeing them but they're not really there. You can think of space but not time. At least you can, but separately. Not time in space.' Walking with her face tipped up she catches her ankle in a root. He holds her and they go up.

Tam has a lantern in the pen. A ewe lies on her side, apparently dead, but as they watch, the stomach, grossly extended between four skinny legs, heaves and flutters. The green eyes of the sheep, still open, seems to observe them. Tam nods:

'I was coming down. But by the time I found her she was near finished.'

'She's gone?'

'Aye.'

'When?' Jesse looks angry. For a second Susan thinks that he might strike Tam.

'Now. A minute. Two maybe.'

'Knife.'

Tam blinks. 'You're going to cut her?'

Jesse has already flung off his coat and is kneeling. He nicks the ewe's belly, then remembers Susan:

'You'd better go back to the house.'

'Can't I help?'

'It'll need feeding, if it lives, till we can find it a ewe. Warm some milk.'

But she stays. Tam holds the lantern and she watches the two men, heads bent. She feels a fool, useless, but is too interested to leave. Then she is appalled as the womb is revealed and Jesse plunges his hands deep in like a woman in dough and pulls out the bloody mess. It's foul and marvellous. He's smiling. She stuffs her knuckles in her mouth and staggers outside to be sick. When she has finished she stays hunched, her cheek against the prickly black grass.

'I told you, get back to the house.' His voice is rough. He keeps his soft face for the lamb. She follows him down the hill.

'How will you get another ewe to take it?'

'Find one with a dead lamb. Skin it. Put the skin on this 'un.'

She stumbles but his arms are full with the lamb. She feels absurdly lonely, excluded, and then is ashamed of herself. Her voice sounds high and artificial:

'You did it so quickly. You seem to know just what to do.'

'I'd better, it's my job.'

'But I'd have no idea . . .'

'It's what you know. Nothing special. Like your reading.'

'But that seems so pointless. It doesn't do anything for anyone but myself. It doesn't save a life.'

'A life?' he says. 'Don't go romancing about it. It's only a beast. I'd kill it as quick for money.' But his face is slanted away from her, towards the sheep, now kicking in his arms. 'You little bogger then, you want to run?' He sets it down and it wobbles in a circle back to him. 'I'm not your mam.' He picks it up again and now they're back at the farm. He says they'll keep it indoors for the night. It's sickly but should live. The honeymoon is over.

She stays outside for a moment in the yard. The racing sky makes the barn topple. There is a scent of hay and salt. She looks up, breasting the waves of darkness, to the high corner of the field where the stars are low and in the pen the lantern glows, a single small outpost of humanity in a scene suddenly cold and by no means benign. She shivers and goes indoors to warm the milk.

**Janice Elliott**

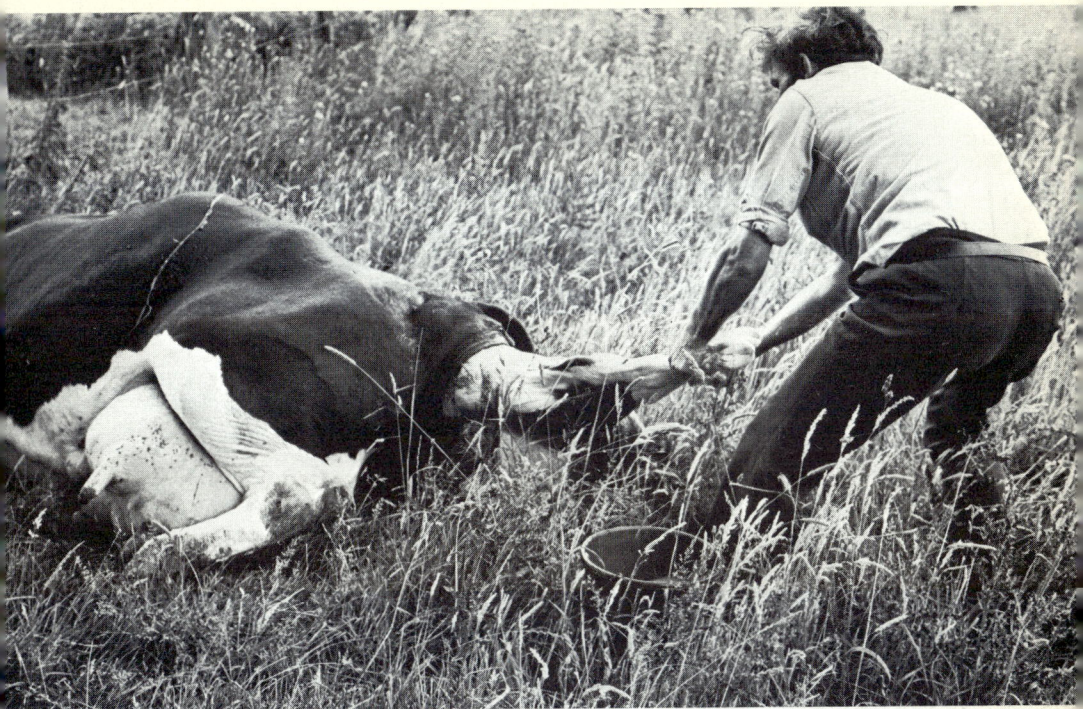

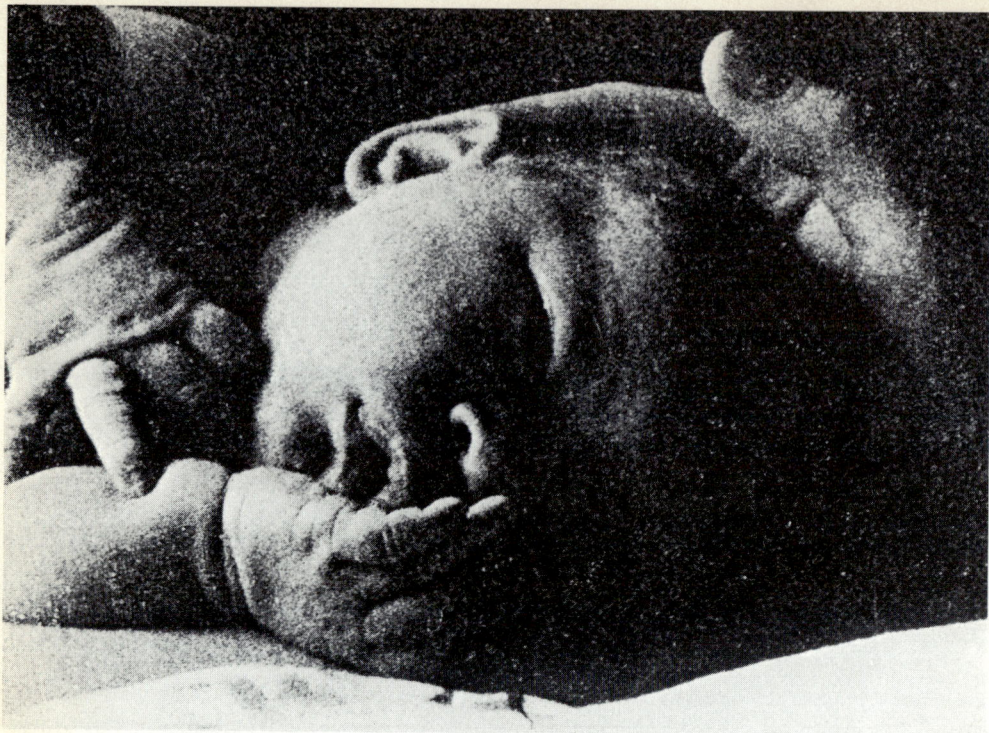

# Birth Without Violence

'Do you believe that birth is an enjoyable experience . . . for the baby?'

'Birth? Enjoyable?'

'You heard me . . . do you believe that babies feel happy coming into this world?'

'You're joking.'

'Why should I be joking?'

'Because babies are just babies.'

'What is that supposed to mean?'

'That babies aren't capable of intense feelings.'

'What makes you so certain?'

'Babies don't have fully developed feelings.'

'How do you *know*?'

'Well, don't you agree?'

'If I did, I wouldn't be asking.'

'But everybody knows they don't.'

'Since when has that ever been a good reason to believe anything?'

'True. But newborn babies can't see or even hear, so how can they feel unhappy?'

'Even if they can't see or hear, that doesn't stop them from crying their hearts out.'

'A baby has to test its lungs. That's common knowledge.'

'Nonsense!'

'Well, that's what people say.'

'People say all kinds of stupid things. But do you really believe that babies feel nothing at all while they're being born?'

'Obviously they don't.'

'I'm not so sure. After all, young children suffer overwhelming agonies about things that seem quite trivial to us – they feel a thousand times more intensely than we do.'

'Yes, I know, but newborn babies are so tiny.'

'What does size have to do with it?'

'Well . . .'

'And why do they scream so loud if they're not in some kind of pain or misery?'

'I don't know – a reflex I suppose. But I'm sure they're not feeling anything.'

'But *why* aren't they?'

'Because they have no conscious awareness.'

'Ah. So you think that means they have no soul.'

'I don't know about the soul.'

'But this consciousness . . . why is it so important?'

'Consciousness is the beginning of being a person.'

'Are you trying to tell me that babies aren't fully human because they're not fully conscious? Tell me more . . .'

How many times have I heard that kind of discussion. It leads nowhere. Things are simple. It's we who complicate them.

When children come into the world, the first thing they do is cry. And everyone relaxes.

'Just listen to that,' the mother exclaims happily, astonished that something so small can make so much noise. Traditionally, this crying means that the reflexes are normal, that the machine works.

But are we machines?

Aren't cries always an expression of pain?

Could it not be that the baby is in anguish?

Could it not be that birth is as painful for the child as giving birth once was for the mother?

And if it is, does anyone care?

I'm afraid, judging by how little consideration we give to a baby, apparently not.

We have a sadly deep-rooted prejudice against believing that this 'thing' can feel, hear or see.

So how could it feel pain?

'It' shrieks, it howls, and that is that.

In short, it is an object.

But what if it were already a *person*?

This first meeting between mother and child is crucial.

Many mothers do not know how to touch their babies. Or, to be more exact, do not dare. They are paralysed.

Many will not admit it, or are not even aware of it. But it is true nevertheless, if you can recognize the signs. Something restrains these mothers, some profound inhibition.

This new body has emerged from what modesty had led us to call, euphemistically, the 'private parts'.

Whatever circumlocution we use, our education has still conditioned most of us to consider these parts of the body as somehow offensive, to reject them; not to mention them.

That's where the baby has come from.

From this region of the body that we are supposed to know nothing about, that we don't examine, that we don't display or touch. That we would deny.

Now this something has emerged from 'there'. Something warm and sticky. And the result of muscular efforts that resemble those we use in excreting.

And it is this 'something' that we must touch!

Moreover, how can we place our hands on something which has just emerged from inside a human stomach? On human entrails.

The mother remains paralysed, frozen by an age-old prohibition.

Suddenly deeply confused, she no longer knows *what* she feels for this 'thing' that is there, on her belly. An immense disgust? A passionate concern?

Sometimes one has to take her hands and place them on the child.

Her resistance is obvious. But once it is overcome, once the step has been taken, the result is extraordinary.

She has transcended the taboo.

The barrier that separated her from her child, and from herself, is down.

She is filled with an indescribable joy.

The old distinction between good and bad, clean and dirty, permissible and forbidden has dissolved.

Suddenly, things are so simple. For the first time in a lifetime!

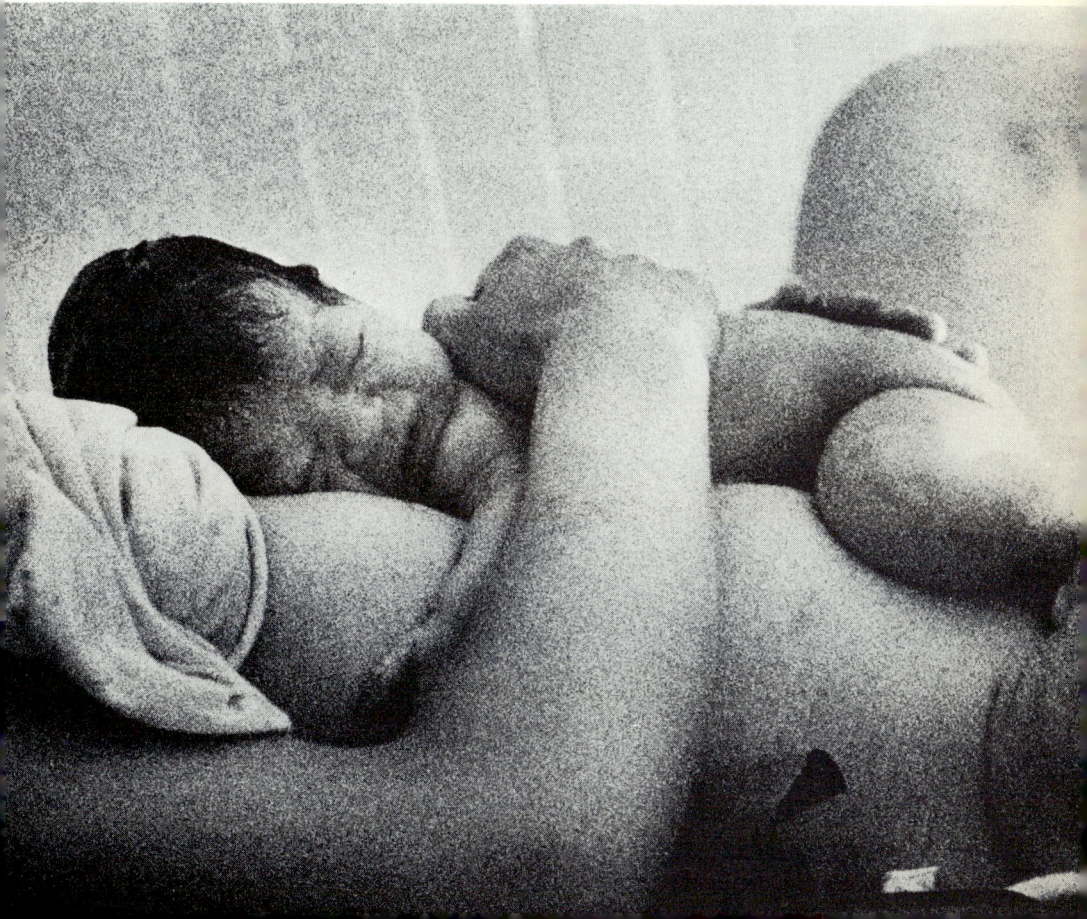

Fear has ebbed.

By touching her child, the woman has at last discovered herself. She had made herself whole.

For her, the internal and the external have been fused.

The hands that touch the child reveal everything to it: nervousness or calm, clumsiness or confidence, tenderness or violence.

The child knows if the hands are loving. Or if they are careless. Or worse, if they are rejecting.

In attentive and loving hands, a child abandons itself, opens out.

In rigid and hostile hands, a child retreats into itself, blocks out the world.

So that before we even think of re-creating the prenatal rhythms which once flowed around this small body, we must let our hands lie on it motionless.

Not hands that are inert, perfunctory, distracted.

But hands that are attentive, alive, alert, responsive to its slightest quiver.

Hands that are light. That neither command nor demand.

That are simply there.
Light . . . and heavy in the weight of tenderness. And of silence.
Whose hands should hold the child? The mother's, of course,
provided that these hands know everything we have been saying.

This cannot be taught, although it can be forgotten.

Many mothers briskly pat their babies! Or shake them, thinking that they're rocking and consoling them . . .

Many have still, lifeless, uncomprehending hands.

Many are so wrapped up in their own emotions that they are literally in danger of smothering their children.

However, in most cases the woman who has delivered her baby naturally will have had to rediscover her own body and to control its ill-timed impulses. So she is ready to hold and touch her baby.

Despite her excitement, she will not overwhelm her child.

When the newborn child is placed on her stomach, when she lays her hands on it, she will think: 'My problems are over. But not my baby's.'

The delivery is over, but the baby's awakening has just begun.

It is on the first step of a wild adventure; it is transfixed with fear.

Do not move. Do not add to the baby's panic.

Just be there. Without moving. Without getting impatient. Without expecting anything.

At this point, out of consideration for her child, out of real – not egocentric – love, a woman will simply place her hands on its body. And leave them there, unmoving. They must give a message not of excitement, agitation and emotion, but of calm and lightness, and of peace.

**Frederic Leboyer**

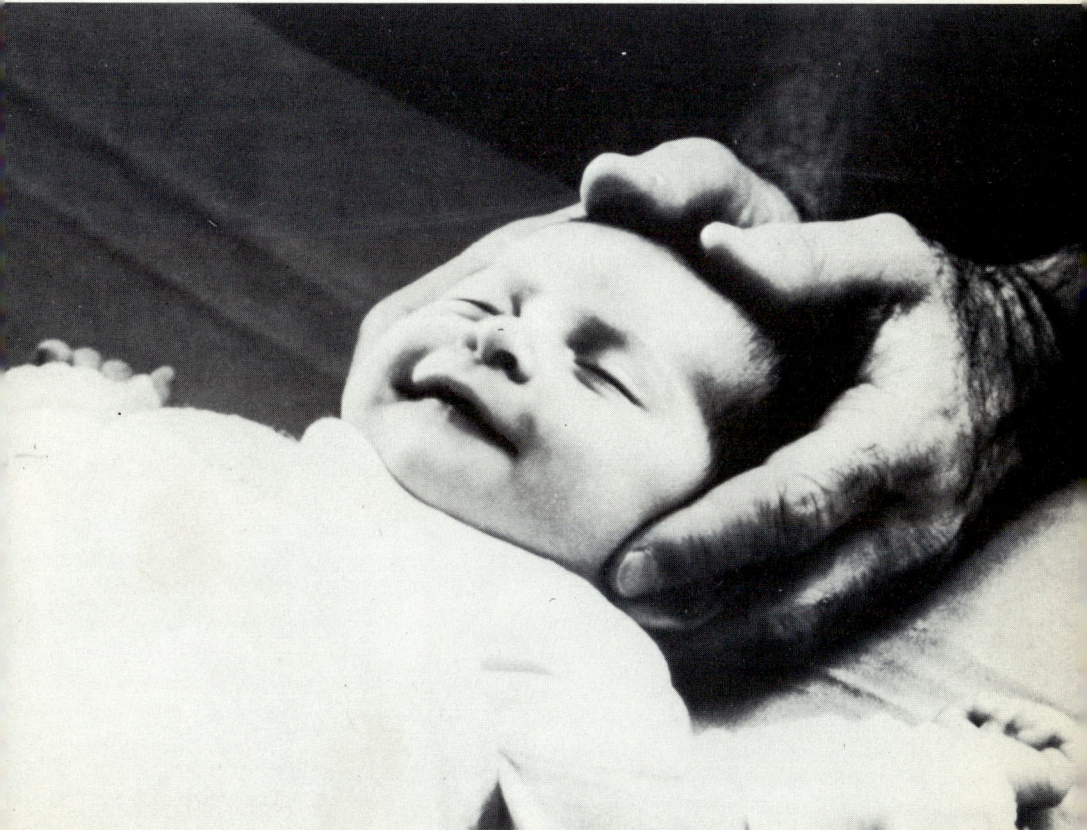

# Wife-Wooing

Oh my love. Yes. Here we sit, on warm broad floorboards, before a fire, the children between us, in a crescent, eating. The girl and I share one half-pint of French-fried potatoes; you and the boy share another; and in the centre, sharing nothing, making simple reflection within himself like a jewel, the baby, mounted in an Easybaby, sucks at his bottle with frowning mastery, his selfish, contemplative eyes stealing glitter from the centre of the flames. And you. You. You allow your skirt, the same black skirt in which this morning you with woman's soft bravery mounted a bicycle and sallied forth to play hymns in difficult keys on the Sunday school's old piano – you allow this black skirt to slide off your raised knees down your thighs, slide *up* your thighs in your body's absolute geography, so the parallel whiteness of their undersides is exposed to the fire's warmth and to my sight. Oh. There is a line of Joyce. I try to recover it from the legendary, imperfectly explored grottoes of *Ulysses*: a garter snapped, to please Blazes Boylan, in a deep Dublin den. What? Smackwarm. That was the crucial word. Smacked smackwarm on her smackable warm woman's thigh. Something like that. A splendid man, to feel that. Smackwarm woman's. Splendid also to feel the curious and potent, inexplicable and irrefutably magical life language leads within itself. What soul took thought and knew that adding 'wo' to man would make a woman? The difference exactly. The wide w, the receptive o. Womb. In our crescent the children for all their size seem to come out of you towards me, wet fingers and eyes, tinted bronze. Three children, five persons, seven years. Seven years since I wed wide warm woman, white-thighed. Wooed and wed. Wife. A knife of a word that for all its final bite did not end the wooing. To my wonderment.

We eat meat, meat I wrested warm from the raw hands of the hamburger girl in the diner a mile away, a ferocious place, slick with savagery, wild with chrome; young predators snarling dirty jokes menaced me, old men reached for me with coffee-warmed paws; I wielded my wallet and won my way back. The fat brown bag of buns was warm beside me in the cold car; the smaller bag holding two tiny cartons of French-fries emitted an even more urgent heat. Back through the black winter air to the fire, the intimate cave, where halloos and hurrahs greeted me, the deer, mouth agape and its cotton throat gushing, stretched dead across my shoulders. And now you, beside the white o of the plate upon which the children discarded with squeals of disgust the rings of translucent onion that came squeezed in the hamburgers – you push your toes an inch closer to the blaze, and the ashy white of the inside of your deep thigh is lazily laid bare, and the eternally elastic garter snaps smackwarm against my hidden heart.

Who would have thought, wide wife, back there in the white tremble of the ceremony (in the corner of my eye I held, despite the distracting hail of ominous vows, the vibration of the cluster of stephanotis clutched against your wrist), that seven years would bring us no distance, through all those warm beds, to the same trembling point, of beginning? The cells change every seven years, and down in the atom, apparently, there is a strange discontinuity; as if God wills the universe anew every instant. (Ah God, dear God, tall friend of my childhood, I will never forget you, though they say dreadful things. They say rose windows in cathedrals are vaginal symbols.) Your legs, exposed as fully as by a bathing suit, yearn deeper into the amber wash of heat. Well: begin. A green jet of flame spits out sideways from a pocket of resin in a log, crying, and the orange shadows on the ceiling sway with fresh life. Begin.

'Remember, on our honeymoon, how the top of the kerosene heater made a great big rose window on the ceiling?'

'Vnn.' Your chin goes to your knees, your shins drawn in, all is retracted. Not much to remember, perhaps, for you; blood badly spilled, clumsiness of all sorts. 'It was cold for June.'

'Mommy, what was cold? What did you say?' the girl asks, enunciating angrily, determined not to let language slip on her tongue and tumble her so that we laugh.

'A house where Daddy and I stayed one time.'

'I don't like dat,' the boy says, and throws a half bun painted with chartreuse mustard onto the floor.

You pick it up with beautiful sombre musing ask, 'Isn't that funny? Did any of the others have mustard on them?'

'I *hate* dat,' the boy insists; he is two. Language is to him thick vague handles swirling by; he grabs what he can.

'Here. He can have mine. Give me his.' I pass my hamburger over, you take it, he takes it from you, there is nowhere a ripple of gratitude. There is no more praise of my heroism in fetching Sunday supper, saving your labour. Cunning, you sense, and sense that I sense your knowledge, that I had hoped to hoard your energy towards a more ecstatic spending. We sense everything between us every ripple, existent and nonexistent; it is tiring. Courting a wife takes tenfold the strength of winning an ignorant girl. The fire shifts, shattering fragments of newspaper that carry in lighter grey the ghosts of the ink of their message. You huddle your legs and bring the skirt back over them. With a sizzling noise like the sighs of the exhausted logs, the baby sucks the last from his bottle, drops it to the floor with its distasteful hoax of vacant suds, and begins to cry. His egotist's mouth opens; the delicate membrane of his satisfaction tears. You pick him up and stand. You love the baby more than me.

Who would have thought, blood once spilled, that no barrier would be broken, that you would be each time healed into a virgin again? Tall, fair, obscure, remote, and courteous.

We put the children to bed, one by one, in reverse order of birth. I am limitlessly patient, paternal, good. Yet you know. We watch the paper bags and cartons ignite on the breathing pillow of embers; read, watch television, eat crackers, it does not matter. Eleven comes. For a tingling moment you stand on the bedroom rug in your underpants, untangling your nightie; oh, fat white sweet fat fatness. In bed you read. About Richard Nixon. He fascinates you; you hate him. You know how he defeated Jerry Voorhis, martyred Mrs Douglas, how he played poker in the Navy despite being a Quaker, every fiendish trick, every low adaptation. Oh my Lord. Let's let the poor man go to bed. We're none of us perfect. 'Hey let's turn out the light.'

'Wait. He's just about to get Hiss convicted. It's very strange. It says he acted honourably.'

'I'm sure he did.' I reach for the switch.

'No. Wait. Just till I finish this chapter. I'm sure there'll be something at the end.'

'Honey, Hiss was guilty. We're all guilty. Conceived in concupiscence, we die unrepentant.' Once my ornate words wooed you.

I lie against your filmy convex back. You read sideways, a sleepy trick. I see the page through the fringe of your hair, sharp and white as a wedge of crystal. Suddenly it slips. The book has slipped from your hand. You are asleep. Oh cunning trick, cunning. In the darkness I consider. Cunning. The headlights of cars accidentally slide fanning slits of light around our walls and ceiling. The great rose window was projected upward through the petal-shaped perforations in the top of the black kerosene stove, which we stood in the centre of the floor. As the flame on the circular wick flickered, the wide soft star of interlocked penumbra moved and waved as if it were printed on a silk cloth being gently tugged or slowly blown. Its colour soft blurred blood. We pay dear in blood for our peaceful homes.

In the morning, to my relief, you are ugly. Monday's wan breakfast light bleaches you blotchily, drains the goodness from your thickness, makes the bathrobe a limp stained tube flapping disconsolately, exposing sallow décolletage. The skin between your breasts a sad yellow. I feast with the coffee on your drabness. Every wrinkle and sickly tint a relief and a revenge. The children yammer. The toaster sticks. Seven years have worn this woman.

The man, he arrows off to work, jousting for right-of-way, veering on the thin hard edge of the legal speed limit. Out of domestic muddle, softness, pallor, flaccidity: into the city. Stone is his province. The winning coin. The manoeuvring of abstractions. Making heartless things run. Oh the inanimate, adamant joys of job!

I return with my head enmeshed in a machine. A technicality it would take weeks to explain to you snags my brain; I fiddle with phrases and numbers all the blind evening. You serve me supper as a waitress – as less than a waitress, for I have known you. The children touch me timidly, as they would a steep girder bolted into a framework whose height they don't understand. They drift into sleep securely. We survive their passing in calm parallelity. My thoughts rework in chronic right angles the same snagging circuits on the same professional grid. You rustle the book about Nixon; vanish upstairs into the plumbing; the bathtub pipes cry. In my head I seem to have found the stuck switch at last: I push at it; it jams; I push it; it is jammed. I grow dizzy, churning with cigarettes, I circle the room aimlessly.

So I am taken by surprise at a turning when at the meaningful hour of ten you come with a kiss of toothpaste to me moist and girlish and quick; the momentous moral of this story being, An expected gift is not worth giving.

**John Updike**

# The River-Merchant's Wife: A Letter

While my hair was still cut straight across my forehead
I played about the front gate, pulling flowers.
You came by on bamboo stilts, playing horse,
You walked about my seat, playing with blue plums.
And we went on living in the village of Chokan:
Two small people, without dislike or suspicion.

At fourteen I married My Lord you.
I never laughed, being bashful.
Lowering my head, I looked at the wall.
Called to, a thousand times, I never looked back.

At fifteen I stopped scowling,
I desired my dust to be mingled with yours
For ever and for ever and for ever.
Why should I climb the look out?

At sixteen you departed,
You went into far Ku-to-yen, by the river of swirling eddies,
And you have been gone five months.
The monkeys make sorrowful noise overhead.

You dragged your feet when you went out.
By the gate now, the moss is grown, the different mosses,
Too deep to clear them away!
The leaves fall early this autumn, in wind.
The paired butterflies are already yellow with August
Over the grass in the West garden;
They hurt me. I grow older.
If you are coming down through the narrows of the river Kiang,
Please let me know beforehand,
And I will come out to meet you
                As far as Cho-fu-Sa.

**Rihaku** *translated by Ezra Pound*

# Those Winter Sundays

Sundays too my father got up early
and put his clothes on in the blueblack cold,
then with cracked hands that ached
from labour in the weekday weather made
banked fires blaze. No one ever thanked him.

I'd wake and hear the cold splintering, breaking.
When the rooms were warm, he'd call,
and slowly I would rise and dress,
fearing the chronic angers of that house,

Speaking indifferently to him,
who had driven out the cold
and polished my good shoes as well.
What did I know, what did I know
of love's austere and lonely offices?

**Robert Hayden**

# Walter Llywach

Walter Llywach! The words were the name
On a lost letter that never came
For one who waited in the long queue
Of life that wound through a Welsh valley.
I took instead, as others had done
Before, a wife from the back pew
In chapel, rather to share the rain
Of winter evenings than to intrude
On her pale body. And yet we lay
For warmth together and laughed to hear
Each new child's cry of despair.

**R. S. Thomas**

# That's How It Was

I sat at the back of the class and waited. Any moment she might call out my name and I'd get up and say it, the poem I'd chosen. Janice was reading now. What had she picked?

'Now more than ever seems it rich to die,
To cease upon the midnight with no pain.'

Poor Janice, she had to hurry home tonight, and couldn't wait for Miss Tyson and walk down the road with her, like we did most days, Janice almost running by her side, Miss Tyson trotting along swinging her little briefcase, me wheeling my bike along the gutter, glancing up to see if she was looking and then hurriedly down at the handlebars as the large grey eyes turned full on me and the low voice asked:

'What do you think, Paddy?'

She was the only one of the staff who called me Paddy, to the rest I was Patricia. I thought of Light-the-long-handed, Lleu-Llaw-gyffes who'd had no soul till he had a name. Nouns – names were the most powerful words. They strike home like the pin through the butterfly – liar, cheat, girl, bastard, king and you're caught wriggling, staked through the heart by an identity, and no matter how much you squirm and protest, 'No it isn't like that,' the noun holds you down till you set fast in the pose it nails you to.

'And what have you chosen, Paddy?'

I stood up a bit dazed.

'Shakespeare, Miss Tyson.'

'Good. A speech from a play?'

'No. A sonnet.' Miss Tyson had given me the little red book of sonnets for my birthday. No one knew, except Janice of course and my mother. I knew many of them by heart already and, in the evening when I went upstairs to bed, I sat at the window in the room that was mine now, watching the sky turn apple-green behind the red-brick council houses and the fields beyond blur into the horizon, and repeated them softly into the twilight, lips hardly moving, the whispered syllables dropping into the stilled air, gentle as the brush of bats' wings against the sky.

'Being your slave, what should I do but tend
Upon the hours and times of your desire?'

The words moved over the hushed room, over the other girls' faces upturned towards me as I spoke. I didn't look at the book in my hands but towards Miss Tyson who sat listening, her head slightly bent.

'Nor dare I question with my jealous thought,
Where you may be, or your affairs suppose,
But, like a sad slave, stay and think of nought
Save where you are how happy you make those.'

'How could she understand?' I thought. No one understood. There were so many ways of loving. I felt my voice beginning to break and dug my nails into the palms of my hands; I crushed my bare knee against the underneath of the desk where the splinters were. The quick pain brought relief and I managed to finish the last couplet in a clear full voice:

'So true a fool is love that in your will'

Miss Tyson raised her head. Was there the ghost of a smile on her face? Maybe she was laughing at me all the time.

'Though you do anything he thinks no ill!'

I ended with head held high.

'Thank you, Paddy. A very good choice.' There was no trace of a smile now.

I sat down dazed. Had she understood? The rest of the lesson passed; I was scarcely conscious of the other voices reading, only of her every movement, every word.

I think I was in love with Evelyn Tyson as soon as I saw her come into the room on that first day at the High School, and three years later I was still in love with her. It hadn't faded as these things are supposed to do, in fact it had grown in intensity until now it was like a fever that occupied my every thought, sleeping and waking, and raged in my blood. Far off I heard the bell ringing. She gathered up her books, I stood up with the rest of the class while she left the room.

After school I hung about in the cloakroom until the prefects turned me out, then in the bicycle shed, ducking when Granny Wright, the senior mistress, and Sergeant-Major came past on their way home, my two worst subjects maths and games. When they were safely by I heaved my bike out of its stand and trundled it up out of the shed into the sun. I propped the front wheel against the gatepost, wandered back along the path and picked a big ox-eye daisy from the tall bouquets of weeds and feathery grasses decorating the door of the shed.

'She loves me, she loves me not.' I stripped off the flat white petals. There was a sound of footsteps, light swinging steps on gravel. I knew the rules of the *amour courtois*, the lady must never be embarrassed. I dropped on one knee beside the bike and fiddled with the back brake-block which could always be relied on to be slightly at fault. The footsteps were nearly up to me; I could hear her breathing and the soft guttural sound as she cleared her throat.

Would she speak or just pass on?

'Hallo, Paddy, trouble with the bike?' Anyone else would have said bicycle. I straightened up, feeling pink in the face from stooping.

'The brakes, but they're alright now.'

'Good.' She began to move away. I took hold of the handlebars and wheeled the bike along beside her.

'I thought you read very well this afternoon.'

'I used your book, the one you gave me.'

'I'm glad it was useful. I thought you'd appreciate it.'

'I understand now why he's considered the greatest poet. I used to think Keats was but he seems sickly sometimes.'

'What did you think of the Koestler?'

'It's wonderful. I've nearly finished it, but it raises so many questions, things I've thought about myself but never seen discussed in a book.'

'Yes. I think I know. What exactly were you thinking of?'

'Well, religion. What do you think about God?'

She laughed. 'An immense subject; we haven't time to go into all that now.'

I looked up. It was true, in a few yards our ways divided. It was always the same: waiting for her, walking beside her, time no longer existed, until we were nearly at the corner and it sprang out on us, wolfing down the last few seconds, tainting the final moments with the sourness of its breath.

'It would need a whole evening for a subject like that and then we should hardly have started.' I held myself still inside for a second, willing her to go on.

'Please God let her say it.' And then the sudden thought, 'You're not sure there is a God any more.'

'Why not come round one evening to tea, and then we can talk it over?' I was willing her so fiercely to say the words that when they came I barely heard them. Perhaps I'd dreamt them. I looked down at her. Her eyes were like grey sea; I felt myself drowning.

'Could I? That'd be marvellous. When could I come?'

'What about tomorrow?'

'Oh yes!'

'You're sure your mother won't mind?'

'Oh no, I'm sure she won't.' But my heart hesitated for a moment. 'What time shall I come?'

'About six, then we'll get tea out of the way early and have plenty of time to talk.'

'I'll bring back the Koestler.' I paused. There was something else I ought to say. 'You're sure it's alright? I'm not taking up your time, not being a nuisance?'

'I don't think so, do you?' She looked at me straight and full. I looked down. I wanted to bother her but I knew the rules. 'Tomorrow then,' she said.

'Until tomorrow.' She turned up the road towards the terrace house where she had rooms. I got on the bike, thrust at the pedals and whirled down the road and over the bridge in wild exultation. At the killer hill I stood up on the pedals and forced my way, foot by foot, up to the top and over the brow.

My mother was standing at the front gate. 'We're out of jam,' she said as I pulled up. 'I've been waiting for you. You'll have to go down to the stores.'

I was exhausted by the effort to beat the hill and cross at everyday concerns intruding on my mood. I'd wanted to go upstairs to my bedroom hugging the thought of tomorrow to myself.

'Oh Lord can't we do without it?'

'No we can't, there's nothing for tea.'

I took the money. 'I wish you'd think of these things in the morning, then I could get them on my way home. I'm tired by the time I get up here.'

'I can't think of everything, and anyway you'd forget all about it during the day. You're too full of other things.' She turned away up the path.

I let the bike take me down the hill. Why bother to brake? Let it run on gathering speed until it collided with one of the big brewer's drays coming out of the bottling store. I sat back on the saddle steering mechanically. That would be that. All problems solved. But the bike seemed to know its own way and reached the bottom safely, slowing gradually as the road flattened. I bought the tin of oversweet pineapple mush and pedalled wearily home. This time I got off at the bottom of the hill and pushed my way to the top.

The table was all laid when I got in. She came to meet me at the door, hearing the scrape of the bike against the outside wall.

'You got it? Good. I was afraid they might be shut.' She opened the tin and spooned gleaming yellow dollops of jam into a jar.

'If you sit down now you can have some butter before the others get in.' She poured the tea and gave me a plate with three thin pieces of bread and butter. I ate slowly, savouring the taste while she told me about her day. The Red Cross had been with a parcel.

'Don't worry, Mrs Willerton,' the lady had said as she delivered it. 'I've seen their curtains twitching as I came in. I know who deserves a parcel. You take no notice of anything they say. They don't know what you have to put up with, just because you're always clean and decent.' And she stamped on the clutch with her heavy brogue and rattled away.

'I thought we could all go to the pictures tomorrow,' she said.

I took a deep breath and said casually: 'I can't. Miss Tyson's invited me to tea.'

'Oh!' I went on eating slowly. 'Oh well, Ted and I can go to the Horseshoe then.' Without me to take her and bring her back she wouldn't go down to the town.

'I can't really refuse now I've said I'll go, can I?'

'No, of course you can't.' But the accent fell on the wrong word somehow. I finished my tea.

'I've got a lot of homework to do.'

'Yes, you'll have to get ahead won't you, for tomorrow.'

I went heavily upstairs, the bread and butter seemed indigestible. They would sit in the pub on the corner, which she disliked because it was modern and characterless, full of the Chinatown neighbours, the Wortbridge swedes we called them.

Sitting on my bed I took out my diary and wrote rather shakily.

*Tomorrow I am going to tea with Evelyn. We shall talk about God and Arthur Koestler, philosophy and art. I shall take her my poems to read. It can never be the same again.*

Then I sat looking at it for a moment, prodding the page with my pencil.

I put the diary away in my drawer and took out my books. I'd have to get stuck into it to finish tomorrow's quota as well. Firmly I kept my mind on the job, only when Venus rose in the opaque sky I opened the window and let the evening in.

   'Bright star, would I were steadfast as thou art'

The words moved out into the calm twilight.

   'Pillow'd upon my fair love's ripening breast,
   To feel forever it's soft fall and swell
   Awake forever in a sweet unrest.'

I scarcely saw her the next day, just a glimpse at the end of the dining-room, then a smile and a thank you as I served her with shepherd's pie. I was afraid she might have changed her mind but, if so, surely she would have told me. I said nothing to Janice; it would have seemed like triumphing.

'I don't need any tea,' I said when I got home. 'I'm having it there.'

'Mind you behave yourself.'

I didn't answer. The imputation made me angry. The house seemed stifling. I couldn't breathe. I washed my hands and face in the sink and went upstairs. I rolled my tie into a short sausage to straighten some of the creases. The cuffs of my blouse were beginning to grey with grime, it was nearly the end of the week, but if I pulled my cardigan well down and kept it on all the time they wouldn't show. I put on my tie and knotted it in the thick part to look less stringy, then combed my hair. I went downstairs.

'I'll have to go now.' She looked up from her book.

'Have a nice time. Mind you're in by ten. Are you taking the bike?'

'Yes.' Every word seemed double-edged.

'Go on then. Don't keep her waiting.' She looked back at the page in front of her. I rode off dispiritedly.

It was a bit early I knew. I circled the block once or twice then drew up outside the house, propped the bike against the kerb and rang the bell. I smoothed my hair nervously while I waited. She was hovering in the doorway behind as her landlady opened the door.

'Come in.'

'Shall I bring supper in now, Miss Tyson?'

'Yes please, if it's ready.' She urged me into her room.

For ten minutes I was lost. I could hardly breathe or speak for my heart, which was like a mad thing in my body, pounding to get out, but she spoke of this and that, easing me into the situation until I was calmer. I sat on the edge of the armchair, clenching and unclenching my hands, while she moved about the room, tidying away books, the letter she'd been writing. Finally she gave me a thick volume and sat down in the opposite chair, draping a cardigan around her shoulders and drawing it close with a characteristic gesture.

'That has a lot of sane answers.' It was the *History of Western Philosophy*. 'Or at least it asks the right questions.'

'And God?'

'He is there or here, we agree on that don't we, but . . .'

'How is He to be worshipped?'

'Yes, that's it exactly.'

There was a knock on the door. She opened it quickly and ushered in the landlady with a loaded tray. We were both a little constrained in front of her waiting for her to go, while she chatted of the weather and the iniquities of the ginger cat stretched on the rug in front of the hearth. She seemed an intruder.

'The wind's getting up. It'll rain before long. If there's anything else you want, Miss Tyson, just let me know.' She closed the door behind her.

'May I call you Evelyn?' Somehow I'd started the sentence before I'd decided to say it and halfway through I realized I had to go on.

'If this is going to happen very often you'd better I think.' It was more than I'd dared hope for.

We ate, me trembling for an errant fork or a clumsy gesture – we never had a tea table so full of hazards at home – Evelyn calm, and accustomed to the galaxy of cutlery. Between forkfuls of smoked haddock she told me something about her home.

'The country is very fine. You must come and see it one day.' And about her childhood. 'I hated school but then there wasn't much at home either. Parents very rarely understand, at least mine didn't. It's a closed world to them, this sort of thing,' she waved her fork towards the wireless that was playing Mozart's 39th Symphony and the open copy of *The Faber Book of Modern Verse* beside it.

I agreed guiltily, thinking of my mother's efforts to keep up with me against the hopeless odds of the Willertons and the circumstances of her life. Outside the wind had risen to a howl and rain thudded against the taut window panes. Inside was a cell of sweetness and light and civilized humanity, that made the rest of my life seem a shrieking chaos.

'If it gets too rough you'll have to stay the night,' she said when the evening was nearly over. What could I say? Desire was so great it became a pain that brought fear.

'I expect it'll stop soon,' I said, matter-of-factly, and we left it like that. I showed her the poems I'd brought with me.

'They're in chronological order starting with the last so you needn't plough all the way through.' Some she'd set herself as homework exercises, mostly the earlier stuff, but the most recent I'd written to her rather than for her. They were copied as neatly as I could, I was never a tidy writer, into an exercise book with stiff maroon covers. While she read I watched. The light fell straight down on to her face, reflecting from the soft down on her cheeks, the full lips and almost cleft chin.

'She isn't even beautiful,' I told myself but my hand longed to go out and trace the curve of cheek and lip.

The concert had finished long ago. I looked at the clock.

'I must go. I have to be in by ten.'

Outside the wind still blew but the sound of rain had stopped.

'I'll lend you a coat.' I wanted to accept but felt I must refuse.

'No it's alright. It's stopped raining I think.' She went to the window and looked out.

'Yes it has.' I was grateful that she didn't insist.

'Good night,' I said at the door. 'And thank you; it's been a wonderful evening.'

'Goodness, don't mention it.' And I laughed inside at the familiar phrase, laughed tenderly because it was her only verbal concession to convention. 'Good night then,' she said. 'Let me know when you want to come again, when you need a change.' Her hand touched mine by accident, just a touch but it seared into the flesh. I turned into the wind and rode off into the dark.

'She might have had the sense to lend you a mac,' my mother said.

**Maureen Duffy**

# Two Young Men, 23 to 24 Years Old

He'd been sitting in the café since ten-thirty
expecting him to turn up any minute.
Midnight had gone, and he was still waiting for him.
It was now after one-thirty, and the cafe was almost deserted.
He'd grown tired of reading newspapers
mechanically. Of his three lonely shillings
only one was left: waiting that long,
he'd spent the others on coffees and brandy.
And he'd smoked all his cigarettes.
So much waiting had worn him out.
Because alone like that for so many hours,
he'd also begun to have disturbing thoughts
about the immoral life he was living.

But when he saw his friend come in –
weariness, boredom, thought all disappeared at once.

His friend brought unexpected news.
He'd won sixty pounds playing cards.

Their good looks, their exquisite youthfulness,
the sensitive love they shared
were refreshed, livened, invigorated
by the sixty pounds from the card table.

Now all joy and vitality, feeling and charm,
they went – not to the homes of their respectable families
(where they were no longer wanted anyway)
– they went to a familiar and very special
house of debauchery, and they asked for a bedroom
and expensive drinks, and they drank again.

And when the expensive drinks were finished
and it was close to four in the morning
happy, they gave themselves to love.

**C. P. Cavafy** *translated by Edmund Keeley*
*and Philip Sherrard*

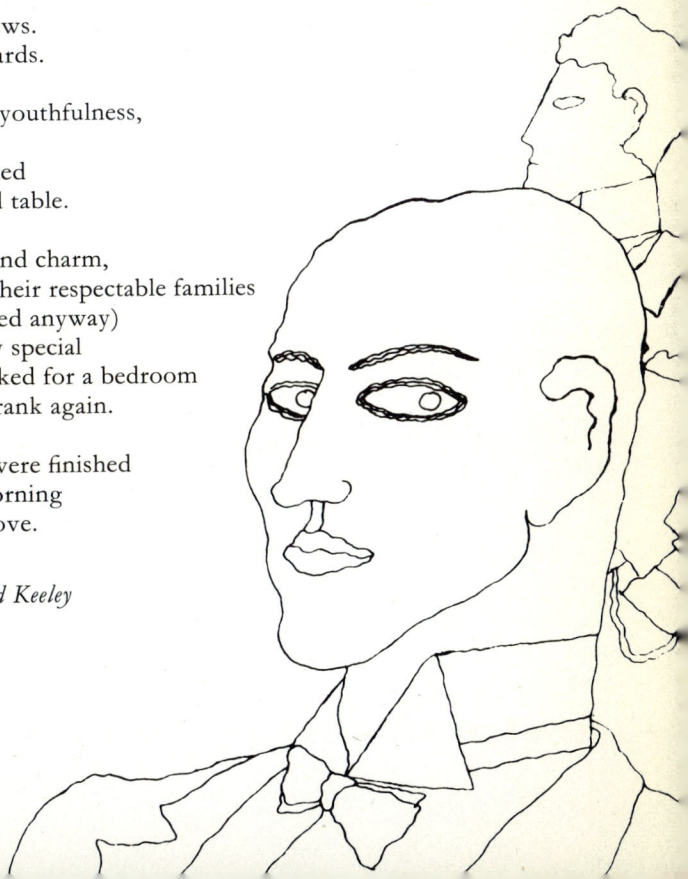

# Andromeda

Consider the problem of chains.
It would appear that Andromeda
Tied to the rock
Waited for our hero to arrive
To cut them.
But sea air is bad for chains
In time they'd rusted badly.
Broken links, small heaps of red dust
Lay around
Unobserved
That is to say, deliberately unobserved
Until
In spite of innumerable
Surreptitious efforts to piece them together
The facts were unavoidable.
They'd crumbled, vanished
Outlived their purpose.
But tendencies for chain-making
Continue to compel.
It was no great problem for one
Accustomed to such matters
To replace the old set with a new
But different . . .
Man-held not rock-held

Chains, chain-making and chain-makers
Are likely to be much affected
By the difference between men and rocks.

**Connie Rosen**

10.11.59.

# Martha and Her Mother

She woke with a start; the bed next to her was empty. There were noises next door. Then she saw it was nearly eleven. While she stood in her nightdress, fumbling at her dressing gown, the door began very gently to open inwards. Its cautious movement was arrested; then the person the other side dropped something; the door crashed back against the wall, and Mrs Quest stumbled into the room, reaching out for parcels which scattered everywhere.

'Oh, so you're up,' Mrs Quest said sharply. 'I didn't mean to wake you. I was coming in quietly.' Then, retrieving a last package to make a neat pile on the bed, she added archly, 'What a dashing life you lead, lying in bed till eleven.'

This roguishness aroused in Martha the usual strong distaste. She had covered herself entirely with her dressing gown, buttoning it up tight from throat to hem.

'I thought you must be ill, I peeped in and saw you. Shall I go for the doctor, don't get up, stay in bed and I'll nurse you – for today, at least.'

'I'm perfectly well,' said Martha ungraciously. 'Let's go and have some tea.' Firmly, she led the way from the bedroom, but Mrs Quest did not follow her at once.

Martha sat on the divan listening. Her mother was following the ritual that she had already gone through here, in this room. The flowers had been removed from their vases and rearranged, the chairs set differently, books put into places. Mrs Quest had reassured herself by touching and arranging everything in the living room, and was now doing the same in the bedroom. Martha had time to make the tea and bring in the tray before her mother reappeared.

'I've just made your bed, your nightdress is torn, did you know? I've brought it to mend while I'm here, your bathroom isn't done, it's wet,' Mrs Quest remarked flurriedly. She had Martha's nightdress clutched in one hand. She glanced at it, blushed, and remarked coquettishly, 'How you can wear these transparent bits of fluff I don't know.'

Martha poured the tea in silence. She was exaggeratedly irritated. The violence of this emotion was what kept her silent; for she was quite able to assure herself that nothing could be more natural, and even harmless and pathetic, than this unfortunate woman's need to lead every other life but her own. This is what her intelligence told her; her conscience remarked that she was making a fuss about nothing; but in fact she seethed with irritation. The face she presented to her mother was one of numbed hostility. This, as usual, affected Mrs Quest like an accusation.

The next phase of this sad cycle followed: Mrs Quest said that it was unfair to Douglas not to sleep enough: she would get ill and then he would have to pay the bills. Martha's face remaining implacable, she went on, in tones of hurried disapproval: 'If you'll give me a needle and thread, I'll mend your nightdress.'

Martha got up, found needle and thread, and handed them to Mrs Quest without a word. The sight of that nightdress, still warm from her own body, clutched with nervous possession in her mother's hands was quite unendurable. She was determined to endure it. After all, she thought, if it gives her pleasure . . . And then: It's not her fault she was brought up in *that* society. This thought gave her comparative detachment. She sat down and looked at the worn, gnarled hands at work on her nightdress. They filled her with pity for her mother. Besides, she could remember how she had loved her mother's hands as a child; she could see the white and beautiful hands of a woman who no longer existed.

Mrs Quest was talking of matters on the farm, about the house in town they were shortly to buy, about her husband's health.

Martha scarcely listened. She was engaged in examining and repairing those intellectual bastions of defence behind which she sheltered, that building whose shape had first been sketched so far back in her childhood she could no longer remember how it then looked. With every year it had become more complicated, more ramified; it was as if she, Martha, were a variety of soft, shell-less creature whose survival lay in the strength of those walls. Reaching out in all directions from behind it, she clutched at the bricks of arguments, the stones of words, discarding any that might not fit into the building.

She was looking at Mrs Quest in a deep abstract speculation, as if neither she nor her mother had any validity as persons, but were mere pawns in the hands of an old fatality. She could see a sequence of events, unalterable, behind her, and stretching unalterably into the future. She saw her mother, a prim-faced Edwardian schoolgirl, confronting, in her case, the Victorian father, the patriarchal father with rebellion. She saw herself sitting where her mother now sat, a woman horribly metamorphosed, entirely dependent on her children for any interest in life, resented by them, and resenting them; opposite her, a young woman of whom she could distinguish nothing clearly but a set, obstinate face; and beside these women, a series of shadowy dependent men, broken-willed and sick with compelled diseases. This the nightmare, this the nightmare of a class and generation: repetition. And although Martha had read nothing of the great interpreters of the nightmare, she had been soaked in the minor literature of the last thirty years, which had dealt with very little else: a series of doomed individuals, carrying their doom *inside* them, like the seeds of fatal disease. Nothing could alter the pattern.

But inside the stern web of fatality did flicker small hopeful flames. One thought was that after all it had not always been that these great life-and-death struggles were fought out inside the family; presumably things might change again. Another was that she had decided not to have a baby; and it was in her power to cut the cycle.

Which brought her back into the conversation with a question on her tongue.

Mrs Quest was talking about the coming war. She had no doubt at all as to the shape it would assume. It was Britain's task to fight Hitler and Stalin combined. Martha suggested that this might be rather a heavy task. Mrs Quest said sharply that Martha had no patriotism, and never had had. Even without those lazy useless Americans who never came into the war until they could make good pickings out of it, Britain would ultimately muddle through to victory, as she always did.

Martha was able to refrain from being *logical* only by her more personal preoccupations. She plunged straight in with an enquiry as to whether her mother had ever had an abortion. She hastened to add that she wanted to know because of a friend of hers.

Mrs Quest, checked, took some moment to adjust to this level. She said vaguely, 'It's illegal . . .' Having made this offering to the law, she considered the question on its merits and said in a lowered voice, a look of distaste on her face, 'Why – are you like that?'

Martha suppressed the hostility she felt at the evasion and said, 'No.'

'Well, you look like it,' said Mrs Quest bluntly, with triumph.

'Well, I'm not.' Martha added the appeal, 'I do wish you'd tell me . . .' She had no idea what she really wanted to know!

Mrs Quest looked at her, her vigorous face wearing the dubious puzzled expression which meant she was trying to remember her own past.

Martha was telling herself that this appeal was doomed to produce all kinds of misunderstandings and discomfort. They always did. And what *did* she want her mother to say? She looked at her in silence, and wished that some miracle would occur and her mother would produce a few simple, straightforward remarks, a few *words* – not emotional, nothing deviating from the cool humorous understatement that would save them both from embarrassment. Martha needed the right words.

She reflected that Mrs Quest had not wanted her. How, then, had she come to accept her? Was that what she wanted to know? But looking at her now, she could only think that Mrs Quest had spent a free, energetic youth, had 'lived her own life' – she had used the phrase herself long before it was proper for middle-class daughters to do so – and had, accordingly, quarrelled with her father. She had not married until very late.

For many years now, she had been this immensely efficient down-to-earth matron; but somewhere concealed in her was the mother who had borne Martha. From her white and feminine body she, Martha, had emerged – that was certainly a fact! She could remember seeing her mother naked; beautiful she had been, a beautiful, strong white body, with full hips, small high breasts – the Greek idea of beauty. And to that tender white body had belonged the strong soft white hands. Martha remembered. Those hands had tended her, the baby. Well, then, why could her mother not resurrect that woman in her and speak the few simple, appropriate words?

But now she was turning Martha's flimsy nightgown between her thickened, clumsy hands, as if determined not to say she disapproved of it; and frowned. She looked uncomfortable. Martha quite desperately held on to that other image to see against this one. She could see that earlier woman distinctly. More, she could feel wafts of tenderness coming from her.

Then, suddenly, into this pure and simple emotion came something new: she felt pity like a clutching hand. She was remembering something else. She was lying in the dark in that house on the farm, listening to a piano being played several rooms away. She got up, and crept through the dark rooms to a doorway. She saw Mrs Quest seated at the keyboard, a heavy knot of hair weighting her head and glistening gold where the light touched it from two candle flames which floated steadily above the long white transparent candles. Tears were running down her face while she set her lips and smiled. The romantic phrases of a Chopin nocturne rippled out into the African night, steadily accompanied by the crickets and the blood-thudding of the tomtoms from the compound. Martha smiled wryly: she could remember the gulf of pity that sight had thrown her into.

Mrs Quest looked up over the nightdress and enquired jealously, 'What are you laughing at?'

'Mother,' she said desperately, 'you didn't want to have me. Well, then . . .'

Mrs Quest laughed, and said Martha had come as a surprise to her.

Martha waited, then prodded, 'What did you *feel*?'

A slight look of caution came on to her mother's honest square face. 'Oh, well . . .' But almost at once she launched into the gay and humorous account, which Martha had so often heard, of the difficulties of getting the proper clothes and so on; which almost at once merged with the difficulties of the birth itself – a painful business, this, as she had so often been told.

'But what did you *feel* about it all? I mean, it couldn't have been as easy as all that,' said Martha.

'Oh, it wasn't easy – I was just telling you,' Mrs Quest began to repeat how awkward a baby Martha had been. 'But it wasn't really your fault. First I didn't have enough milk, though I didn't know it; and then I gave you a mixture, and didn't know until the doctor told me that it was only half the right strength. So in one way and another I half starved you for the first nine months of your life.' Mrs Quest laughed ruefully, and said, 'No wonder you never stopped crying day or night.'

A familiar resentment filled Martha, and she at once pressed on. 'But, Mother, when you first knew you were going to have a baby –'

Mrs Quest interrupted. 'And then I had your brother, he was such a good baby, not like you.'

And now Martha abdicated, as she had so often done before; for it had always, for some reason, seemed right and inevitable that Mrs Quest should prefer the delicate boy child to herself. Martha listened to the familiar story to the end, while she suppressed a violent and exasperated desire to take her mother by the shoulders and shake her until she produced, in a few sensible and consoling sentences, that truth which it was so essential Martha should have. But Mrs Quest had forgotten how she felt. She was no longer interested. And why should she be, this elderly woman with all the business of being a woman behind her?

**Doris Lessing** *A Proper Marriage*

# Together We are Building a Wall

Together we are building a wall
to keep us apart;
a high, translucent wall
through which we see each other
clearly but without comprehension.
I build with pride and aloneness
and mine is a wall of desolation.
I think you have not seen our wall yet.

**Sara O'Reilly**

# My Father in the Night Commanding No

My Father in the night commanding No
Has work to do. Smoke issues from his lips;
   He reads in silence.
The frogs are croaking and the street lamps glow.

And then my mother winds the gramophone;
The Bride of Lammermoor begins to shriek –
   Or reads a story
About a prince, a castle and a dragon.

The moon is glittering above the hill.
I stand before the gateposts of the King –
    So runs the story –
Of Thule, at midnight when the mice are still.

And I have been in Thule! It has come true –
The journey and the danger of the world,
    And all that there is
To bear and to enjoy, endure and do.

Landscapes, seascapes . . . where have I been led?
The names of cities – Paris, Venice, Rome –
    Held out their arms.
A feathered God, seductive, went ahead.

Here is my house. Under a red rose tree
A child is swinging; another gravely plays.
    They are not surprised
That I am here; they were expecting me.

And yet my father sits and reads in silence.
My mother sheds a tear, the moon is still,
    And the dark wind
Is murmuring that nothing ever happens.

Beyond his jurisdiction as I move
Do I not prove him wrong? and yet, it's true
    *They* will not change
There, on the stage of terror and of love.

The actors in that playhouse always sit
In fixed positions – father, mother, child
    With painted eyes.
How sad it is to be a little puppet!

Their heads are wooden. And you once pretended
To understand them! Shake them as you will,
    They cannot speak.
Do what you will, the comedy is ended.

Father, why did you work? Why did you weep,
Mother? Was the story so important?
    '*Listen*!' the wind
Said to the children, and they fell asleep.

**Louis Simpson**

# The Stone Boy

Arnold drew his overalls and ravelling grey sweater over his naked body. In the other narrow bed his brother Eugene went on sleeping, undisturbed by the alarm clock's rusty ring. Arnold, watching his brother sleeping, felt a peculiar dismay; he was nine, six years younger than Eugie, and in their waking hours it was he who was subordinate. To dispel emphatically his uneasy advantage over his sleeping brother, he threw himself on the hump of Eugie's body.

'Get up! Get up!' he cried.

Arnold felt his brother twist away and saw the blankets lifted in a great wing, and, all in an instant, he was lying on his back under the covers with only his face showing, like a baby, and Eugie was sprawled on top of him.

'Whassa matter with you?' asked Eugie in sleepy anger, his face hanging close.

'Get up,' Arnold repeated. 'You said you'd pick peas with me.'

Stupidly, Eugie gazed around the room as if to see if morning had come into it yet. Arnold began to laugh derisively, making soft, snorting noises, and was thrown off the bed. He got up from the floor and went down the stairs, the laughter continuing, like hiccups, against his will. But when he opened the staircase door and entered the parlour, he hunched up his shoulders and was quiet because his parents slept in the bedroom downstairs.

Arnold lifted his .22-calibre rifle from the rack on the kitchen wall. It was an old lever-action Winchester that his father had given him because nobody else used it any more. On their way down to the garden he and Eugie would go by the lake, and if there were any ducks on it he'd take a shot at them. Standing on the stool before the cupboard, he searched on the top shelf in the confusion of medicines and ointments for man and beast and found a small yellow box of .22 cartridges. Then he sat down on the stool and began to load his gun.

It was cold in the kitchen so early, but later in the day, when his mother canned the peas, the heat from the wood stove would be almost unbearable. Yesterday she had finished preserving the huckleberries that the family had picked along the mountain, and before that she had canned all the cherries his father had brought from the warehouse in Corinth. Sometimes, on these summer days, Arnold would deliberately come out from the shade where he was playing and make himself as uncomfortable as his mother was in the kitchen by standing in the sun until the sweat ran down his body.

Eugie came clomping down the stairs and into the kitchen, his head drooping with sleepiness. From his perch on the stool Arnold watched Eugie slip on his green knit cap. Eugie didn't really need a cap; he hadn't had a haircut in a long time and his brown curls grew thick and matted, close around his ears and down his neck, tapering there to a small whorl. Eugie passed his left hand through his hair before he set his cap down with his right. The very way he slipped his cap on was an announcement of his status; almost everything he did was a reminder that he was eldest – first he, then Nora, then Arnold – and called attention to how tall he was (almost as tall as his father), how long his legs were, how small he was in the hips, and what a neat dip above his buttocks his thick-soled logger's boots gave him. Arnold never tired of watching Eugie offer silent praise unto himself. He wondered, as he sat enthralled, if when he got to be Eugie's age he would still be undersized and his hair still straight.

Eugie eyed the gun. 'Don't you know this ain't duck season?' he asked gruffly, as if he were the sheriff.

'No, I don't know.' Arnold said with a snigger.

Eugie picked up the tin washtub for the peas, unbolted the door with his free hand and kicked it open. Then, lifting the tub to his head, he went clomping down the back steps. Arnold followed, closing the door behind him.

The sky was faintly grey, almost white. The mountains behind the farm made the sun climb a long way to show itself. Several miles to the south, where the range opened up, hung an orange mist, but the valley in which the farm lay was still cold and colourless.

Eugie opened the gate to the yard and the boys passed between the barn and the row of chicken houses, their feet stirring up the carpet of brown feathers dropped by the moulting chickens. They paused before going down the slope to the lake. A fluky morning wind ran among the shocks of wheat that covered the slope. It sent a shimmer northward across the lake, gently moving the rushes that formed an island in the centre. Killdeer, their white markings flashing, skimmed the water, crying their shrill, sweet cry. And there at the south end of the lake were four wild ducks, swimming out from the willows into open water.

Arnold followed Eugie down the slope, stealing, as his brother did, from one shock of wheat to another. Eugie paused before climbing through the wire fence that divided the wheatfield from the marshy pasture around the lake. They were screened from the ducks by the willows along the lake's edge.

'If you hit your duck, you want me to go in after it?' Eugie said.

'If you want.' Arnold said.

Eugie lowered his eyelids, leaving slits of mocking blue. 'You'd drown 'fore you got to it, them legs of yours are so puny,' he said.

He shoved the tub under the fence and, pressing down the centre wire, climbed through into the pasture.

Arnold pressed down the bottom wire, thrust a leg through and leaned forward to bring the other leg after. His rifle caught on the wire and he jerked at it. The air was rocked by the sound of the shot. Feeling foolish, he lifted his face, baring it to an expected shower of derision from his brother. But Eugie did not turn around. Instead, from his crouching position, he fell on his knees and then pitched forward onto his face. The ducks rose up crying from the lake, cleared the mountain background and beat away northward across the pale sky.

Arnold squatted beside his brother. Eugie seemed to be climbing the earth, as if the earth ran up and down, and when he found he couldn't scale it he lay still.

'Eugie?'

Then Arnold saw it, under the tendril of hair at the nape of the neck – a slow rising of bright blood. It had an obnoxious movement, like that of a parasite.

'Hey, Eugie,' he said again. He was feeling the same discomfort he had felt when he had watched Eugie sleeping; his brother didn't know that he was lying face down in the pasture.

Again he said 'Hey, Eugie,' an anxious nudge in his voice. But still Eugie was as still as the morning about them.

Arnold set his rifle on the ground and stood up. He picked up the tub and, dragging it behind him, walked along the willows to the garden fence and climbed through. He went down on his knees among the tangled vines. The pods were cold with the night, but his hands were strange to him, and not until some time had passed did he realize that the pods were numbing his fingers. He picked from the top of the vine first, then lifted the vine to look underneath for pods and then moved on to the next.

It was a warmth on his back, like a large hand laid firmly there, that made him raise his head. Way up the slope the grey farmhouse was struck by the sun. While his head had been bent the land had grown bright around him.

When he got up his legs were so stiff that he had to go down on his knees again to ease the pain. Then, walking sideways, he dragged the tub, half full of peas, up the slope.

The kitchen was warm now; a fire was roaring in the stove with a closed-up, rushing sound. His mother was spooning eggs from a pot of boiling water and putting them into a bowl. Her short brown hair was uncombed and fell forward across her eyes as she bent her head. Nora was lifting a frying pan full of trout from the stove, holding the handle with a dish towel. His father had just come in from bringing the cows from the north pasture to the barn, and was sitting on the stool, unbuttoning his red plaid Macknaw.

'Did you boys fill the tub?' his mother asked.

'They ought to by now,' his father said. 'They went out of the house an hour ago. Eugie woke me up comin' downstairs. I heard you shootin' – did you get a duck?'

'No,' Arnold said. They would want to know why Eugie wasn't coming in for breakfast, he thought. 'Eugie's dead,' he told them.

They stared at him. The pitch cracked in the stove.

'You kids playin' a joke?' his father asked.

'Where's Eugene?' his mother asked scoldingly. She wanted, Arnold knew, to see his eyes, and when he had glanced at her she put the bowl and spoon down on the stove and walked past him. His father stood up and went out of the door after her. Nora followed them with little skipping steps, as if afraid to be left alone.

Arnold went into the barn, down along the foddering passage past the cows waiting to be milked, and climbed into the loft. After a few minutes he heard a terrifying sound coming towards the house. His parents and Nora were returning from the willows, and sounds sharp as knives were rising from his mother's breast and carrying over the sloping fields. In a short while he heard his father go down the back steps, slam the car door and drive away.

Arnold lay still as a fugitive, listening to the cows eating close by. If his parents never called him, he thought, he would stay up in the loft forever, out of the way. In the night he would sneak down for a drink of water from the faucet over the trough and for whatever food they left for him by the barn.

The rattle of his father's car as it turned down the lane recalled him to the present. He heard voices of his Uncle Andy and Aunt Alice as they and his father went past the barn to the lake. He could feel the morning growing heavier with sun. Someone, probably Nora, had let the chickens out of their coops and they were cackling in the yard.

After a while another car turned down the road off the highway. The car drew to a stop and he heard the voices of strange men. The men also went past the barn and down to the lake. The undertakers, whom his father must have phoned from Uncle Andy's house, had arrived from Corinth. Then he heard everybody come back and heard the car turn around and leave.

'Arnold!' It was his father calling from the yard.

He climbed down the ladder and went out into the sun, picking wisps of hay from his overalls.

Corinth, nine miles away, was the county seat. Arnold sat in the front seat of the old Ford between his father, who was driving, and Uncle Andy; no one spoke. Uncle Andy was his mother's brother, and he had been fond of Eugie because Eugie had resembled him. Andy had taken Eugie hunting and had given him a knife and a lot of things, and now Andy, his eyes narrowed, sat tall and stiff beside Arnold.

Arnold's father parked the car before the courthouse. It was a two-storey brick building with a lamp on each side of the bottom step. They went up the wide stone steps, Arnold and his father going first, and entered the darkly panelled hallway. The shirt-sleeved man in the sheriff's office said that the sheriff was at Carlson's Parlour examining the Curwing boy.

Andy went off to get the sheriff while Arnold and his father waited on a bench in the corridor. Arnold felt his father watching him, and he lifted his eyes with painful casualness to the announcement, on the opposite wall, of the Corinth County Annual Rodeo, and then to the clock with its loudly clucking pendulum. After he had come down from the loft his father and Uncle Andy had stood in the yard with him and asked him to tell them everything, and he had explained to them how the gun had caught on the wire. But when they had asked him why he hadn't run back to the house to tell his parents, he had had no answer – all he could say was that he had gone down into the garden to pick the peas. His father had stared at him in a pale, puzzled way, and it was then that he had felt his father and the others set their cold, turbulent silence against him. Arnold shifted on the bench, his only feeling a small one of compunction imposed by his father's eyes.

At a quarter past nine Andy and the sheriff came in. They all went into the sheriff's private office, and Arnold was sent forward to sit in the chair by the sheriff's desk; his father and Andy sat down on the bench against the wall.

The sheriff lumped down into his swivel chair and swung toward Arnold. He was an old man with white hair like wheat stubble. His restless green eyes made him seem not to be in his office but to be hurrying and bobbing around somewhere else.

'What did you say your name was?' the sheriff asked.

'Arnold,' he replied; but he could not remember telling the sheriff his name before.

'Curwing?'

'Yes.'

'What were you doing with a .22, Arnold?'

'It's mine,' he said.

'Okay. What were you going to shoot?'

'Some ducks,' he replied.

'Out of season?'

He nodded.

'That's bad,' said the sheriff. 'Were you and your brother good friends?'

What did he mean – good friends? Eugie was his brother. That was different from a friend, Arnold thought. A best friend was your own age, but Eugie was almost a man. Eugie had had a way of looking at him, slyly and mockingly and yet confidentially, that had summed up how they both felt about being brothers. Arnold had wanted to be with Eugie more than with anybody else but he couldn't say they had been good friends.

'Did they ever quarrel?' the sheriff asked his father.

'Not that I know,' his father replied. 'It seemed to me that Arnold cared a lot for Eugie.'

'Did you?' the sheriff asked Arnold.

If it seemed so to his father, then it was so. Arnold nodded.

'Were you mad at him this morning?'

'No.'

'How did you happen to shoot him?'

'We was crawlin' through the fence.'

'Yes?'

'An' the gun got caught on the wire.'

'Seems the hammer must of caught,' his father put in.

'All right, that's what happened,' said the sheriff. 'But what I want you to tell me is this. Why didn't you go back to the house and tell your father right away? Why did you go and pick peas for an hour?'

Arnold gazed over his shoulder at his father, expecting his father to have an answer for this also. But his father's eyes, larger and even lighter blue than usual, were fixed upon him curiously. Arnold picked at a callous in his right palm. It seemed odd now that he had not run back to the house and wakened his father, but he could not remember why he had not. They were all waiting for him to answer.

'I come down to pick peas,' he said.

'Didn't you think,' asked the sheriff, stepping carefully from word to word, 'that it was more important for you to go tell your parents what had happened?'

'The sun was gonna come up,' Arnold said.

'What's that got to do with it?'

'It's better to pick peas while they're cool.'

The sheriff swung away from him, laid both hands flat on his desk. 'Well, all I can say is,' he said across to Arnold's father and Uncle Andy, 'he's either a moron or he's so reasonable that he's way ahead of us.' He gave a challenging snort. 'It's come to my notice that the most reasonable guys are mean ones. They don't feel nothing.'

For a moment the three men sat still. Then the sheriff lifted his hand like a man taking an oath. 'Take him home,' he said.

Andy uncrossed his legs. 'You don't want him?'

'Not now,' replied the sheriff. 'May be in a few years.'

Arnold's father stood up. He held his hat against his chest. 'The gun ain't his no more,' he said wanly.

Arnold went first through the hallway, hearing behind him the heels of his father and Uncle Andy striking the floor boards. He went down the steps ahead of them and climbed into the back seat of the car. Andy paused as he was getting into the front seat and gazed back at Arnold, and Arnold saw that his uncle's eyes had absorbed the knowingness from the sheriff's eyes. Andy and his father and the sheriff had discovered what made him go down into the garden. It was because he was cruel, the sheriff had said, and didn't care about his brother. Was that the reason? Arnold lowered his eyelids meekly against his uncle's stare.

The rest of the day he did his tasks around the farm, keeping apart from the family. At evening, when he saw his father stomp tiredly into the house, Arnold did not put down his hammer and leave the chicken coop he was repairing. He was afraid that they did not want him to eat supper with them. But in a few minutes another fear that they would go to the trouble of calling him and that he would be made conspicuous by his tardiness made him follow his father into the house. As he went through the kitchen he saw the jars of peas standing in rows on the workbench, a reproach to him.

No one spoke at supper, and his mother, who sat next to him, leaned her head in her hand all through the meal, curving her fingers over her eyes so as not to see him. They were finishing their small, silent supper when the visitors began to arrive, knocking hard on the back door. The men were coming from their farms now that it was growing dark and they could not work any more.

Old Man Matthews, grey and stocky, came first, with his two sons, Orion, the elder, and Clint, who was Eugie's age. As the callers entered the parlour, where the family ate, Arnold sat down in a rocking chair. Even as he had been undecided before supper whether to remain outside or take his place at the table, he now thought that he should go upstairs, and yet he stayed to avoid being conspicuous by his absence. If he stayed, he thought, as he always stayed and listened when visitors came, they would see that he was only Arnold and not the person the sheriff thought he was. He sat with his arms crossed and his hands tucked into his armpits and did not lift his eyes.

The Matthews men had hardly settled down around the table, after Arnold's mother and Nora had cleared away the dishes, when another car rattled down the road and someone else rapped on the back door. This time it was Sullivan, a spare and sandy man, so nimble of gesture and expression that Arnold had never been able to catch more than a few of his meanings. Sullivan, in dusty jeans, sat down in the other rocker, shot out his skinny legs and began to talk in his fast way, recalling everything that Eugene had ever said to him. The other men interrupted to tell of occasions they remembered, and after a time Clint's young voice, hoarse like Eugene's had been, broke in to tell about the time Eugene had beat him in a wrestling match.

Out in the kitchen the voices of Orion's wife and Mrs Sullivan mingled with Nora's voice but not, Arnold noticed, his mother's. Then dry little Mr Cram came, leaving large Mrs Cram in the kitchen, and there was no chair left for Mr Cram to sit in. No one asked Arnold to get up and he was unable to rise. He knew that the story had got around to them during the day about how he had gone and picked peas after he had shot his brother, and he knew that although they were talking only about Eugene they were thinking about him and if he got up, if he moved even his foot, they would all be alerted. Then Uncle Andy arrived and leaned his tall, lanky body against the doorjamb and there were two men standing.

Presently Arnold was aware that the talk had stopped. He knew without looking up that the men were watching him.

'Not a tear in his eye,' said Andy and Arnold knew that it was his uncle who had gestured the men to attention.

'He don't give a hoot, is that how it goes?' asked Sullivan, trippingly.

'He's a reasonable fellow,' Andy explained. 'That's what the sheriff said. It's us who ain't reasonable. If we'd of shot our brother, we'd of come runnin' back to the house, cryin' like a baby. Well, we'd of been unreasonable. What would of been the use of actin' like that? If your brother is shot dead, he's shot dead. What's the use of gettin' emotional about it? The thing to do is go down to the garden and pick peas. Am I right?'

The men around the room shifted their heavy, satisfying weight of unreasonableness.

Matthews' son Orion said: 'If I'd done what he done, Pa would've hung my pelt by the side of that big coyote's in the barn.'

Arnold sat in the rocker until the last man had filed out. While his family was out in the kitchen bidding the callers good night and the cars were driving away down the dirt lane to the highway, he picked up one of the kerosene lamps and slipped quickly up the stairs. In his room he undressed by lamplight, although he and Eugie had always undressed in the dark, and not until he was lying in his bed did he blow out the flame. He felt nothing, not any grief. There was only the same immense silence and crawling inside of him; it was the way the house and fields felt under a merciless sun.

He awoke suddenly. He knew that his father was out in the yard, closing the doors of the chicken houses so that the chickens could not roam out too early and fall prey to the coyotes that came down from the mountains at daybreak. The sound that had wakened him was the step of his father as he got up from the rocker and went down the back steps. And he knew that his mother was awake in her bed.

Throwing off the covers, he rose swiftly, went down the stairs and across the dark parlour to his parents' room. He rapped on the door.

'Mother?'

From the closed room her voice rose to him, a seeking and retreating voice. 'Yes?'

'Mother?' he asked insistently. He had expected her to realize that he wanted to go down on his knees by her bed and tell her that Eugie was dead. She did not know it yet, nobody knew it, and yet she was sitting up in bed, waiting to be told, waiting for him to confirm her dread. He had expected her to tell him to come in, to allow him to dig his head into her blankets and tell her about the terror he had felt when he had knelt beside Eugie. He had come to clasp her with his arms and, in his terror, to pommel her breasts with his head. He put his hand upon the knob.

'Go back to bed, Arnold,' she called sharply.

But he waited.

'Go back! Is night when you get afraid?'

At first he did not understand. Then, silently, he left the door and for a stricken moment stood by the rocker. Outside everything was still. The fences, the shocks of wheat seen through the window before him were so still it was as if they moved and breathed in the daytime and had fallen silent with the lateness of the hour. It was a silence that seemed to observe his father, a figure moving alone around the yard, his lantern casting a circle of light by his feet. In a few minutes his father would enter the dark house, the lantern still lighting his way.

Arnold was suddenly aware that he was naked. He had thrown off his blankets and come down the stairs to tell his mother how he felt about Eugie, but she had refused to listen to him and his nakedness had become unpardonable. At once he went back up the stairs, fleeing from his father's lantern.

At breakfast he kept his eyelids lowered as if to deny the humiliating night. Nora, sitting at his left, did not pass the pitcher of milk to him and he did not ask for it. He would never again, he vowed, ask them for anything, and he ate his fried eggs and potatoes only because everybody ate meals – the cattle ate, and the cats; it was customary for everybody to eat.

'Nora, you gonna keep that pitcher for yourself?' his father asked.

Nora lowered her head unsurely.

'Pass it on to Arnold,' his father said.

Nora put her hands in her lap.

His father picked up the metal pitcher and set it down at Arnold's plate.

Arnold, pretending to be deaf to the discord, did not glance up but relief rained over his shoulders at the thought that his parents recognized him again. They must have lain awake after his father had come in from the yard: had they realized together why he had come down the stairs and knocked at their door?

'Bessie's missin' this morning,' his father called out to his mother, who had gone into the kitchen. 'She went up the mountain last night and had her calf, most likely. Somebody's got to go up and find her 'fore the coyotes get the calf.'

That had been Eugie's job, Arnold thought. Eugie would climb the cattle trails in search of a newborn calf and come down the mountain carrying the calf across his back, with the cow running down along behind him, mooing in alarm.

Arnold ate the few more forkfuls of his breakfast, put his hands on the edge of the table and pushed back his chair. If he went for the calf he'd be away from the farm all morning. He could switch the cow down the mountain slowly, and the calf would run along at its mother's side.

When he passed through the kitchen his mother was setting a kettle of water on the stove. 'Where you going?' she asked awkwardly.

'Up to get the calf,' he replied, averting his face.

'Arnold?'

At the door he paused reluctantly, his back to her, knowing that she was seeking him out, as his father was doing, and he called upon his pride to protect him from them.

'Was you knocking at my door last night?'

He looked over his shoulder at her, his eyes narrow and dry.

'What'd you want?' she asked humbly.

'I didn't want nothing,' he said flatly.

Then he went out the door and down the back steps, his legs trembling from the fright his answer gave him.

**Gina Berriault**

# Two Clocks

There was a clock in Grandad's house:
black, gold-numbered,
and a three-foot pendulum.
I'd hear it tick out endless Christmasses,
fingering patches on the green velvet.

Such splendour. *His* chair.
*His* knife. *His* fork. 'Wait!'
Grandma would say,
'til your father gets in!'
Twisting my mother to a girl again.

Revenge needs time. 'That junk,'
my mother said,
and burned the clock,
the velvet, the Blessed Are the Pure in Heart
in red and gold behind the bed.

And brought him back to live with us,
where bleak electric hands swirled gently,
slicing her days and his
into thin fragments.

**John Daniel**

# Norma

*The woman is seated alone in the shelter in the park. She is huddled up in a raincoat and stares out into the middle distance. After a few moments she speaks aloud to herself as in answering a question.*

WOMAN That's all very well but . . . oh no, you couldn't say that, it sounds soft.

MAN (*voice off*) Darling! Darling!

*The woman looks in the direction of the voice then waves and smiles.*

WOMAN Sod you, mate!

*The man runs into the shelter from the rain, he is excited and happy.*

MAN I'm terribly sorry.

WOMAN (*looking at him*) You're very wet.

MAN (*shaking himself*) I'd no idea of the time.

WOMAN Is it warm enough to take your coat off?

MAN (*dabbing his face dry*) And I ran all the way.

WOMAN Well, you would through all that rain, wouldn't you?

*For the first time the man really notices her.*

MAN (*smiling at her*) Yes, I did.

*He sits beside her and takes her hand and speaks with romantic concern.*

MAN Well – how are you?

WOMAN (*moving slightly*) I'd take that coat off if I was you and give it a good shaking.

MAN (*gallantly*) It doesn't matter.

WOMAN (*edgily*) I would have thought it did – it's only showerproof.

MAN Oh, I don't know . . .

WOMAN It is, Roy's got one just like it.

MAN But this is French.

WOMAN (*primly*) Oddly enough so is Roy's.

MAN What's the matter?

WOMAN What do you mean?

MAN Nothing, just what's the matter?

WOMAN I don't know what you're talking about.

MAN Will it be better – I mean, all right if I take my coat off and shake it?

WOMAN Well, that's up to you. Summer showers lead to summer colds, the worst sort, they drag on and there's nothing worse than a cold in August. I had one two years ago – ruined the holiday – Roy got it in the end.

MAN (*astonished*) I don't believe it.

WOMAN (*rattling on*) Perfectly true – Fuengirola – both of us with the sniffles in Fuengirola. He was marvellous about it actually considering I gave the wretched cold to him in the first place.

MAN (*quietly*) Shut up!

WOMAN What?

MAN I said, 'Shut up', Norma, what's going on?

WOMAN Nothing's going on, I was just warning you, that's all.

MAN You were warning me all right, but what about though, 'cos I'm bloody sure it's got nothing to do with this coat, but I'll have it off straight away if that's what you want.

WOMAN That's up to you, I was just . . .

MAN (*interrupting her*) . . . warning me, I know.

*He takes off the offending coat and gives it a vigorous shaking then turns back to her.*

MAN Well?

*She rises.*

WOMAN Let me stretch it out – oh no, there's a nail thing there. (*She indicates a place.*) If I can hang it up it'll drip down. They dry quite quickly.

MAN (*grimly*) Even in the damp?

WOMAN Yes, the material is specially treated – Impermeable – see, it says so on the label.

*He grabs her and kisses her, she is pretty limp. They break.*

WOMAN Somebody's told Roy.

MAN Oh.

WOMAN Yeah – oh.

MAN When did this happen?

WOMAN Some time last week, I don't know – he didn't eat much lunch yesterday so I knew there was something up.

*This expression irritates the man.*

MAN Up?

WOMAN Well, wrong – he usually eats a good lunch on Sundays.

MAN I suppose Roy's eating arrangements *are* important.

WOMAN In this case, very.

MAN I would of thought his knowing had the edge on his failure to gobble down his usual wodge of roast and Yorkshire, but you'd know best.

WOMAN (*tartly*) I ought to, I'm married to the man.

*There is a hostile pause.*

MAN (*contrite*) I'm sorry, I really am.

WOMAN (*contrite*) I had to tell you in my own way, that's all.

MAN Of course you did.

WOMAN He just sat there and looked at it.

MAN The meal?

WOMAN Yeah . . . he sighed.

MAN Sighed?

WOMAN Yeah, a sort of a little sigh.

MAN And?

WOMAN He said, 'Ah well' and pushed the plate away. Of course I knew then something was up – I mean wrong.

MAN So what did you do?

WOMAN I cleared the plate away and went into the kitchen, I was pretty shaken, I can tell you.

MAN I can see. Did he say anything?

WOMAN Not then.

MAN Just gave you the silent treatment?

WOMAN Yes. Anyway, I went up to bed after I'd washed the dishes.

MAN What for?

WOMAN I always wash the dishes so I don't have to face them afterwards.

MAN (*fascinated*) After what?

WOMAN (*matter of fact*) We always go to bed on Sunday afternoons.

MAN Do you?

WOMAN Of course – it's one of the few times Roy isn't too tired.

MAN (*echoing*) Too tired?

WOMAN To make love.

MAN Oh.

WOMAN What's the matter?

MAN Nothing – it's – I didn't think you still –

WOMAN Made love with Roy? Of course I do, I live with him, I'm married to him.

MAN All right, don't go on about it! – Well, obviously nothing happened yesterday.

WOMAN Yes it did.

MAN A row?

WOMAN Yes, after.

MAN After?

WOMAN After we made love.

MAN Oh.

WOMAN He was lying there smoking.

MAN You don't have to draw a picture, you know.

WOMAN I'm just telling you what happened.

MAN All right, all right . . . what happened?

WOMAN He just said, 'You've been committing adultery, haven't you, Norma?'

MAN Christ!

WOMAN I was a bit surprised myself, after all, we'd just been . . .

MAN (*stopping her*) Yes, I know, so of course you denied it.

WOMAN No I didn't, I said 'Yes, dear.'

MAN Oh, Peachy!

WOMAN Well, I was comfy and relaxed and wasn't really thinking.

MAN Did he make a scene?

WOMAN No, he got up and sat by the window looking out.

MAN What happened next?

WOMAN I must have dozed off.

MAN Dozed off!!

WOMAN Not for long.

MAN The time is irrelevant, you dozed off.

WOMAN Well, I was tired, it's been a long week.

MAN I can't believe it.

WOMAN He was still sitting by the window – he had his pyjamas on now. I went over to him. He was staring out at the rain.

MAN That bloody monsoon out there, you mean.

WOMAN I touched him on the leg – it was cold. He looked at me as if he was surprised I was there. Then it happened.

MAN What happened?

WOMAN He started to cry.

MAN Playing for sympathy.

WOMAN He didn't sob or anything, he just cried, the tears just came out and went down his face, it was a bit sad.

MAN What did you do?

WOMAN I got him his dressing-gown and pyjama trousers, he had his slippers on.

MAN I mean, what did you say?

WOMAN Nothing, I couldn't think of anything to say – so I just did things.

MAN Did you get him a drink?

WOMAN It was only half past four, I went downstairs and made the tea.

MAN Just like that?

WOMAN That's the way it was and I couldn't change it.

MAN You didn't even try.

WOMAN Making the tea seemed to be the right thing to do so I made it.

MAN Did he come down?

WOMAN I called him and he came – he was dressed. I thought I'd better explain.

MAN Didn't you ask him how he found out?

WOMAN No – that didn't seem to matter – well, I'd admitted it so I could hardly go back on it, could I?

MAN Did he mention me?

WOMAN No.

MAN Did you mention me?

WOMAN No, he wasn't – well , he didn't seem that interested in who it was and it's not as if you know each other.

MAN (*slightly indignant*) Well, I've seen him about.

WOMAN Oh, he did ask if it was anyone he knew and I think he was glad he didn't know who it was – no – he didn't seem to care who it was once he knew he didn't know him.

MAN Well, I care.

WOMAN Why?

MAN Why? Well, I'm involved too, you know. Was he angry?

WOMAN He was more hurt, he didn't like looking at me, I felt I'd offended him.

MAN Well, you have,

WOMAN But I'd never thought of it like that.

MAN (*accusingly*) You don't sound as if you thought about it at all.

WOMAN Well all right, I hadn't really.

MAN Well what were you thinking about then?

WOMAN It was nice to be with a man who only wanted to please me and play with me. Lots of fun and no responsibilities – like a separate holiday, you must know what I mean?

MAN Sorry, I don't.

WOMAN Well, I certainly didn't want to hurt Roy, why should I? I like him.

MAN But what about me?

WOMAN You? – Oh, well, you've enjoyed it, haven't you?

MAN Sure but I love you.

WOMAN Does that mean you stop enjoying it?

MAN No but it means it's a bit more serious than you are making it sound.

WOMAN But I've got serious at home – I just wanted fun.

MAN God, I thought I meant a little more to you than fun.

WOMAN Why are you knocking fun? Fun was what I hadn't got and for the past two months you've been giving me what I hadn't got, I'm very grateful.

MAN My pleasure.

WOMAN I hope so – but it's got to stop.

MAN What!

WOMAN Oh yes, it's got to stop.

MAN Why?

WOMAN Roy said it aloud, now I can see it.

MAN What?

WOMAN Adultery.

MAN But you said it was fun.

WOMAN Not for Roy.

MAN Well, he better make his own arrangements.

WOMAN No, you don't understand, I didn't mean to hurt him.

MAN What about me?

WOMAN No, it's Roy I've got to think about.

MAN Why, suddenly why have you got to think about him?

WOMAN 'Cos he doesn't like it.

MAN What's 'it'? – go on define 'it'.

WOMAN My doing adultery with you – it hurts him and anything that hurts people is wrong.

MAN I'll be hurt if you stop.

WOMAN Yes, I'm sorry but then I'm married to Roy.

MAN But don't I mean anything to you?

WOMAN Of course you do, you're fun and you made me happy all the time I was with you but Roy's real.

MAN And I'm not, I'm just fun.

WOMAN Yes. We enjoy saying we love each other but we don't mean it, we . . .

MAN (*interrupting her*) I mean it.

WOMAN I'm glad you think you do. No, you see, I've got too much time on my hands, it's been the same ever since the kids went to school and we could afford a daily. I kept on getting bored and restless and Roy was tired. Well, I can't do much other than being a girl and I found myself getting languorous.

MAN Languorous?

WOMAN Yes – like that in the afternoons and Roy's so busy expanding the business I wanted someone to help me.

MAN God, you don't half choose the wrong words – you were using me.

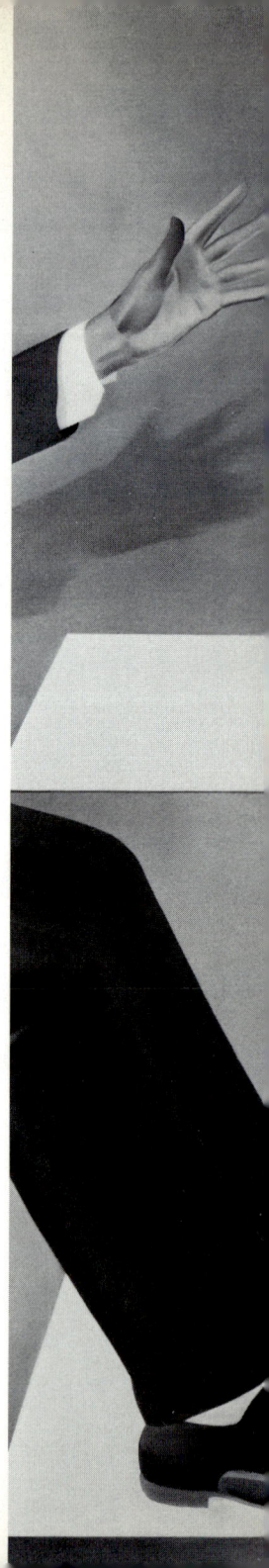

WOMAN Was I? I hadn't thought that much about it. I couldn't make do with books and stuff so when we met – I loved you following me, I loved that most, the way you followed me every afternoon, it was terrible.

MAN What was terrible about it, you attracted me.

WOMAN Oh, I know that but it was delicious, it excited me but I was being selfish so I've got to stop it.

MAN And it hasn't occurred to you you're being selfish now. What about me?

WOMAN You haven't cried. I knew it was wrong when Roy cried – he's not the sort to cry and when he did, I knew I'd hurt him, I told him I only did it to feel a bit more alive. He said, 'But you have to go so near to someone to do it.' That's what hurt him most, he likes me near him, he thinks being near is very important. I think he's probably right so goodbye. I've got to get home for tea.

*She runs off quickly into the rain, leaving the man. It takes him a moment before he realizes what has happened then he shouts after her.*

MAN Norma! Norma! Norma!

**Alun Owen**

# Song for Last Year's Wife

Alice, this is my first winter
of waking without you, of knowing
that you, dressed in familiar clothes
are elsewhere, perhaps not even
conscious of our anniversary. Have
you noticed? The earth's still as hard,
the same empty gardens exist? It is
as if nothing special had changed.
I wake with another mouth feeding
from me, but still feel as if
love had not the right
to walk out of me. A year now. So
what? you say. I send out my spies
to find who you are living with, what
you are doing. They return, smile
and tell me your body's as firm,
you are as alive, warm and inviting
as when they knew you first.
         Perhaps it is the winter,
its isolation from other seasons, that
sends me your ghost to witness
when I wake. Somebody came here today, asked
how you were keeping, what you were doing.
I imagine you, waking in another city,
touched by this same hour. So
ordinary a thing as loss comes now
and touches me.

**Brian Patten**

# Tonight I Write Sadly

Tonight I write sadly.

Write, for example: 'Little grasshopper, shelter from the midnight frost in the scarecrow's sleeve', advising myself.

The night wind throbs in the sky.
Tonight I write so wearily.
Write for example: 'I wanted her, and at times it was me she wanted.'
Write: 'The rain we watched last fall,
Has it fallen this year too?'

She wanted me and at times it was her I wanted.
Yet, it has gone, that want – what's more, I do not care.
It is more terrible than my despair over losing her.

The night always vast, grows enormous without her
And my comfortless tongue talking about her is like a red fox
barred by ivory.

Well, does it matter I loved too weak to keep her?
The night ignores such trivial disputes.

She is not here; that is all.

Far off someone is singing and, as if to bring her back,
I look and run to the end of the road and shout, shout her name.
My voice comes back the same, but weaker.

This night is the same night. It whitens the same tree,
Casts the same shadows. It is as dark, as long, as deep
And as endurable as any other night.

It's true, I don't want her, but perhaps, I want her.
Love is not so brief that I forget her so.

Nevertheless, I shall forget her and alas, as if by accident,
The day will pass in which I do not think about her even once.

And this, the last line I shall write her.

**Pablo Neruda** *translated by Christopher Logue*

# At the Draper's

'I stood at the back of the shop, my dear,
  But you did not perceive me.
Well, when they deliver what you were shown
  *I* shall know nothing of it, believe me!'

And he coughed and coughed as she paled and said,
  'O, I didn't see you come in there –
Why couldn't you speak?' – 'Well I didn't. I left
  That you should not notice I'd been there.

'You were viewing some lovely things. "*Soon required*
  *For a widow, of latest fashion*";
And I knew 'twould upset you to meet the man
  Who had to be cold and ashen

'And screwed in a box before they could dress you
  "*In the last new note in mourning*",
As they defined it. So, not to distress you,
  I left you to your adorning.'

**Thomas Hardy**

# A Very Easy Death

Poupette slept at my place. At ten in the morning we went back to the clinic: as in hotels, the room had to be vacated before noon. Once again we climbed the stairs, opened the two doors: the bed was empty. The walls, the window, the lamps, the furniture, everything was in its place; and on the whiteness of the sheet there was nothing. Foreseeing is not knowing: the shock was as violent as though we had not expected it at all. We took the suitcases out of the cupboard and piled in the books, linen, toilet things, papers: six weeks of an intimacy rotted by betrayal. We left the red dressing-gown behind. We crossed the garden. Somewhere at the bottom, hidden in the greenery, there was a mortuary and inside it Maman's body with the bandage round its chin. Poupette had suffered – by her own desire and also by chance – the hardest blows, and she was too overcome for me to suggest that we should go and see it again. And I was not sure that I wanted to.

We left the suitcases at the rue Blomet, with the concierge. We noticed an undertaker's. 'This will do as well as anywhere else.' Two gentlemen in black asked to know our wishes. They showed us photographs of various kinds of coffin. 'This one is more aesthetic.' Poupette burst into sobbing laughter. 'More aesthetic! That box! She didn't want to be put into that box!' The burial was fixed for Friday, in two days' time. Did we want flowers? We said yes, without knowing why: not a wreath, not a cross, but a big sheaf. Very good: they would take care of everything. In the afternoon we took the suitcases up to the flat: Mademoiselle Leblon had transformed it: it was so much cleaner and more cheerful that we scarcely recognized it – so much the better. We stuffed the bag with the bedjacket and the nightdress in it into a chest of drawers, put the books on a shelf, threw away the eau de Cologne, the sweets and the toilet things, and carried the rest to my place. That night I could not get off to sleep. I was not sorry that I had left Maman with 'I am glad you have seen me looking so well' as her last words. But I did reproach myself for having abandoned her body too soon. She, and my sister too, said, 'A corpse no longer means anything.' Yet it was her flesh, her bones, and for some time still her face. With my father I had stayed by him until the time he became a mere thing for me: I tamed the transition between presence and the void. With Maman I went away almost immediately after having kissed her, and that was why it seemed to me that it was still her that was lying, all alone, in the cold of the mortuary. The coffining would take place in the afternoon of the next day: would I go?

I was at the nursing-home at about four, to pay the bill. Post had arrived for Maman, and a bag of fruit bon-bons. I went up to say goodbye to the nurses. I found the girls, Martin and Parent, very jolly in the corridor. My throat was constricted and I could barely force out a couple of words. I went past the doors of 114: they had taken down the notice 'No Visitors'. In the garden I hesitated for a moment: my courage failed me: and what was the point anyhow? I went away. I saw Cardin's again, and the beautiful dressing-gowns. I told myself that I should never sit in the lobby again, never pick up the white telephone, never make that journey any more: I should so happily have broken with those habits if Maman had been cured, but I still had a nostalgia for them, since it was in losing her that I lost them.

We wanted to give keepsakes to her closest friends. As we looked at her straw bag, filled with balls of wool and an unfinished piece of knitting, and at her blotting-pad, her scissors, her thimble, emotion rose up and drowned us. Everyone knows the power of things: life is solidified by them, more immediately present than in any one of its instants. They lay there on my table, orphaned, useless, waiting to turn into rubbish or to find another identity – my hussif, that Aunt Françoise left me. We set aside her watch for Marthe. As she undid the black ribbon Poupette began to cry. 'It's so stupid and I'm not at all a worshipper of things, but I just can't throw this ribbon away.' 'Keep it.' It is useless to try to integrate life and death and to behave rationally in the presence of something that is not rational: each must manage as well as he can in the tumult of his feelings. I can understand all last wishes and the total absence of them: the hugging of the bones or the abandonment of the body of the one you love to the common grave. If my sister had wanted to dress Maman or to keep her wedding-ring I should certainly have accepted her reactions as willingly as my own. We did not have to ask ourselves questions about the funeral. We felt we knew what Maman wanted and we kept to that.

But we came up against some macabre difficulties. We owned a perpetual concession in the Père-Lachaise cemetery, bought a hundred and thirty years before by a lady named Mignot, our great-grandfather's sister. She was buried there, as well as our grandfather, his wife, his brother, my uncle Gaston and Papa. There was no room left. In such cases the dead person is buried in a provisional grave, and when the bones of those who have been buried before are gathered into a single coffin, then there is a reburial in the family vault. Only as ground in the cemetery is very valuable the management does its best to get the perpetual concessions back into its own hands: it insists that the owner should reaffirm his rights every thirty years. This period had elapsed. We had not been notified in due time that we ran the danger of losing our rights and we therefore still had them – on condition that there was no descendant of the Mignots who might dispute our possession. Until such time as a lawyer should have provided proofs of this, Maman's body would be kept in a repository.

We dreaded the next day's ceremony. We took tranquillizers, slept until seven, drank some tea, ate, and took more tranquillizers. A little before eight a black motor-hearse stopped in the deserted street: before dawn it had gone to fetch the corpse, which had been taken out of the nursing-home by a side-door. We walked through the cold morning fog; we took our seats, Poupette between the driver and one of the Messieurs Durand, I at the back, next to a kind of metal locker. 'Is she there?' asked my sister. 'Yes.' She gave a short sob: 'The only comfort I have,' she said, 'is that it will happen to me too. Otherwise it would be too unfair.' Yes. We were taking part in the dress rehearsal for our own burial. The misfortune is that although everyone must come to this, each experiences the adventure in solitude. We never left Maman during those last days which she confused with convalescence and yet we were profoundly separated from her.

As we drove across Paris I looked at the streets and the people, carefully thinking of nothing. There were cars waiting at the gates of the cemetery: the family. They followed us as far as the chapel. Everybody got out. While the undertaker's men were bringing out the coffin I drew Poupette over towards Maman's sister, whose face was red and swollen with grief. We went in, making a procession: the chapel was full of people. No flowers on the catafalque: the undertakers had left them in the hearse – it did not matter.

A young priest, wearing trousers under his chasuble, celebrated the mass and gave a short, strangely sad sermon. 'God is very far away,' he said. 'Even for those among you whose faith is the strongest there are days when God is so far that He seems not to be there. One might almost say careless. But He has sent us His son.' Two kneeling-chairs had been placed for communion. Almost everybody communicated. The priest spoke again, briefly. And emotion seized both of us by the throat when he said, 'Françoise de Beauvoir'; the words brought her to life; they summed up her history, from birth to marriage, to widowhood, to the grave; Françoise de Beauvoir – that retiring woman, so rarely named – became an important person.

People went by in a line; some of the women were crying. We were still shaking hands when the undertaker's men took the coffin out of the chapel; this time Poupette saw it and she collapsed on my shoulder. 'I had promised her that she shouldn't be put into that box!' I congratulated myself that she did not have the other prayer to remember – 'Don't let me fall into the hole!' One of the Messieurs Durand explained to the people there that now they might go away – it was over. The hearse moved off all by itself; I do not even know where it went.

In a blotting-pad that I had brought back from the clinic I found two lines on a narrow piece of paper, written by Maman in a hand as stiff and firm as when she was twenty: 'I should like a very

simple funeral. No flowers or wreaths. But a great many prayers.'
Well, we had carried out her last wishes, and all the more faithfully
since the flowers had been forgotten.

**Simone de Beauvoir** *translated by Patrick O'Brian*

# The Bustle in a House

The Bustle in a House
The Morning after Death
Is solemnest of industries
Enacted upon Earth –

The Sweeping up the Heart
And putting Love away
We shall not want to use again
Until Eternity

**Emily Dickinson**

# Breaking the News

Do you know those dreadful little places where you keep wondering why the railway ever built a station there; where infinity seems to have congealed over a handful of dirty houses and a dilapidated factory, with fields on all sides condemned to eternal sterility; where you are suddenly aware that they are without hope because there is not a tree, not even a steeple, in sight? The man with the red cap – at last, at last, he gives the signal for the train to pull out – vanishes beneath a signboard bearing an imposing name, and you feel he is paid just to sleep twelve hours a day under a blanket of boredom. A grey horizon is draped over bleak fields cultivated by no one.

Yet I was not the only person to get out; an old woman carrying a large brown-paper parcel stepped down from the next compartment, but by the time I had emerged from the grimy little station she had disappeared as if swallowed up by the ground, and for a moment I was at a loss, not knowing whom to ask for directions. The scattering of brick houses with their dead windows and yellowish-green curtains defied all idea of human habitation, and at right angles to this token street ran a black wall that seemed on the point of collapse. I walked towards this grim-looking wall, afraid to knock at one of the houses of the dead. Then I turned the corner, and next to the grubby, barely legible sign saying 'Inn', I read the words 'Main Road' in clear, neat white lettering on a blue ground. A few more houses forming a crooked façade, crumbling plaster, and on the opposite side, long and windowless, the dingy factory wall like a barricade to the land of desolation. Following my instinct I turned left, but here the place suddenly came to an end; the wall continued for another ten yards or so, then came a leaden-grey field with a barely visible shimmer of green; somewhere the field merged with the grey, limitless horizon, and I had the terrible feeling that I was standing at the end of the world on the brink of a bottomless abyss, as if condemned to be dragged down into that silent, sinister, irresistible undertow of utter hopelessness.

On my left was a small, squat cottage, the kind workmen build in their spare time; I swayed, stumbled, towards it. Passing through a pitiful little gate with a leafless briar rose growing above it, I saw the number, and knew I had come to the right house.

The faded green shutters, their paint long washed away by the rain, were firmly closed, as if glued tight; the low roof – I could reach the gutter with my hand – had been patched with rusty corrugated sheets. The silence was absolute: it was the hour when twilight pauses for breath before welling up, grey and inexorable, over the edge of the horizon. I hesitated for a moment or two at the front door, wishing I had died in '45 when . . . instead of standing here about to enter this house. Just as I was going to raise my hand to knock, I heard a cooing sound, a woman's laugh, from inside; that mysterious, indefinable laugh that, depending on our mood, can either soothe us or wring our hearts. Only a woman who was not alone could laugh like that: again I hesitated, and again the burning, rending desire rose up in me to plunge into the grey infinity of the falling twilight that now hung over the broad fields and was beckoning, beckoning me . . . and with my last ounce of strength I pounded on the door.

First silence, then whispers – and footsteps, soft, slippered footsteps; the door opened, and I saw a fair, pink-cheeked woman who immediately put me in mind of that kind of indescribable radiance that illumines the farthest corners of a shadowy Rembrandt. Golden-red she glowed like a lamp before my eyes in this eternity of grey and black.

With a low cry she stepped back, holding the door open with trembling hands, but when I had taken off my army cap and said, hoarsely, 'Good evening,' the rigid lines of fear slackened in that strangely shapeless face, and she smiled uneasily and said, 'Yes.' In the background a muscular male figure loomed up and melted into the obscurity of the narrow passage. 'I'd like to see Frau Brink,' I said in a low voice. 'Yes,' the woman repeated tonelessly, and nervously pushed open the door. The male figure disappeared in the gloom. I entered a small room, crammed with shabby furniture, where the odour of bad food and excellent cigars seemed to have settled permanently. Her white hand went up to the switch: now that the light fell on her she seemed pale and amorphous, almost corpselike, only her fair, reddish hair was alive and warm. Her hands still trembling, she clutched her dark-red dress to her heavy breasts although it was closely buttoned – almost as if she were afraid I might stab her. The look in her watery blue eyes was wary, alarmed, as if certain that some terrible sentence was awaiting her, she were facing a judge. Even the cheap sentimental prints seemed to have been stuck on the walls like indictments.

'Don't be alarmed,' I said, my voice tense, and instantly I knew that was the worst way I could possibly have chosen to begin, but before I could go on she said, in a strangely composed voice: 'I know all about it, he's dead . . . dead.' I could only nod. I reached into my pocket to hand over his few belongings, but in the passage a furious voice shouted 'Gitta!' She looked at me in despair, then flung open the door and called out shrilly: 'For God's sake, can't you wait five minutes – ?' and banged the door shut again, and I could picture the man slinking off into a corner. Her eyes looked up defiantly, almost triumphantly, into mine.

I slowly placed the wedding ring, the watch, and the paybook with the well-thumbed photograph on the green plush tablecloth. Suddenly she started to sob, wild, terrible cries like an animal's. The outlines of her face dissolved, became soft and shapeless like a slug, and shining teardrops gushed out between her short fleshy fingers. She collapsed onto the sofa, leaning on the table with her right hand while with her left she fingered the pathetic little objects. Memory seemed to be lacerating her with a thousand words. I knew then that the war would never be over, never, as long as somewhere a wound it had inflicted was still bleeding.

I threw aside everything – disgust, fear, and desolation – like a contemptible burden and placed my hand on the plump, heaving shoulder, and as she turned her astonished face towards me I saw for the first time a resemblance to that photo of a pretty, smiling girl that I had had to look at so many hundreds of times, in '45 when . . .

'Where was it – please sit down – on the Russian front?' I could see she was liable to burst into tears again at any moment.

'No, in the West, in the prisoner-of-war camp – there were more than a hundred thousand of us . . .'

'And when?' Her gaze was wide and alert and extraordinarily alive, her whole face tense and young – as if her life depended on my reply. 'In July '45,' I said quietly.

She seemed to reflect for a moment, then she smiled – a pure and innocent smile, and I guessed why she was smiling.

Suddenly I felt as if the house were threatening to collapse about my ears, and I got up. Without a word she opened the door, she wanted to hold it open for me but I waited obstinately until she had gone ahead; and when she gave me her pudgy little hand she said, with a dry sob: 'I knew it, I knew it, when I saw him off – it's almost three years ago now – when I saw him off at the station,' and then she added almost in a whisper: 'Don't despise me.'

I felt a spasm of pain at these words – good God, surely I didn't look like a judge? And before she could stop me I had kissed her small, soft hand: it was the first time in my life I had ever kissed a woman's hand.

Outside darkness had fallen and, as if still under the spell of fear, I paused for a moment by the closed door. Then I heard her sobbing inside, loud, wild sobs, she was leaning against the front door with only the thickness of the wood between us, and at that moment I did indeed long for the house to collapse about her and bury her.

Then, slowly and very, very carefully – for I was afraid of sinking any moment into an abyss – I groped my way back to the station. Lights were twinkling in the houses of the dead, the tiny place seemed to have grown in all directions. I could even see small lamps beyond the black wall that seemed to be illuminating vast expanses of yard. Dusk had become dense and heavy, foggy, vaporous, and impenetrable.

In the draughty little waiting-room there was only an elderly couple standing close together, shivering, in one corner. I waited a long time, my hands in my pockets, my cap pulled down over my ears, for there was a cold draught blowing in from the tracks, and night was falling lower, lower, like an enormous weight.

'If only there were a little more bread, and a bit of tobacco,' muttered the man behind me. And I kept leaning forward to peer along the parallel lines of tracks as they converged in the distance between dim lights.

Suddenly the door was flung open, and the man with the red cap, his face a picture of eager devotion to duty, shouted out, as if he had to make his voice carry across the waiting-room of a great railway station: 'Train for Cologne – ninety-five minutes late!'

At that moment I felt as if I had been taken prisoner for the rest of my life.

**Heinrich Böll** *translated by Leila Vennewitz*

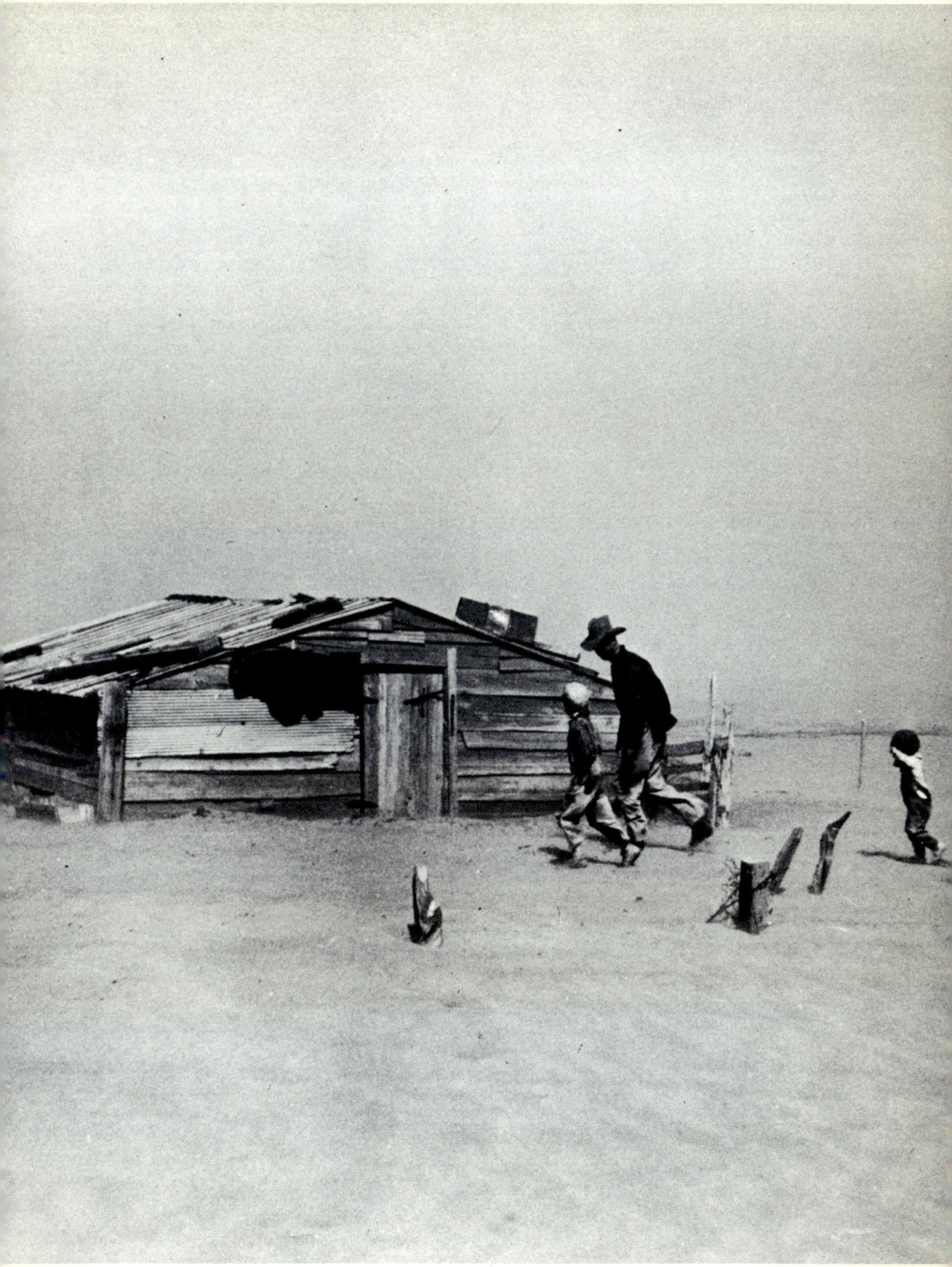

# The Grapes of Wrath

In the little houses the tenant people sifted their belongings and the belongings of their fathers and of their grandfathers. Picked over their possessions for the journey to the west. The men were ruthless because the past had been spoiled, but the women knew how the past would cry to them in the coming days. The men went into the barns and sheds.

That plough, that harrow, remember in the war we planted mustard? Remember a fella wanted us to put in that rubber bush they call guayule? Get rich, he said. Bring out those tools – get a few dollars for them. Eighteen dollars for the plough, plus freight – Sears Roebuck.

Harness, carts, seeders, little bundles of hoes. Bring 'em out. Pile 'em up. Load 'em in the wagon. Take 'em to town. Sell 'em for what you can get. Sell the team and the wagon, too. No more use for anything.

Fifty cents isn't enough to get for a good plough. That seeder cost thirty-eight dollars. Two dollars isn't enough. Can't haul it all back – well, take it, and a bitterness with it. Take the well pump and the harness. Take halters, collars, hames, and tugs. Take the little glass brow-band jewels, roses red under glass. Got those for the bay gelding. 'Member how he lifted his feet when he trotted?

Junk piled up in a yard.

Can't sell a hand plough any more. Fifty cents for the weight of the metal. Disks and tractors, that's the stuff now.

Well, take it – all junk – and give me five dollars. You're not buying only junk, you're buying junked lives. And more – you'll see – you're buying bitterness. Buying a plough to plough your own children under, buying the arms and spirits that might have saved you. Five dollars, not four. I can't haul 'em back – well, take

'em for four. But I warn you, you're buying what will plough your own children under. And you won't see. You can't see. Take 'em for four. Now, what'll you give for the team and wagon? Those fine bays, matched they are, matched in colour, matched the way they walk, stride to stride. In the stiff pull – straining hams and buttocks, split-second timed together. And in the morning, the light on them, bay light. They look over the fence sniffing for us, and the stiff ears swivel to hear us, and the black forelocks! I've got a girl. She likes to braid the manes and forelocks, puts little red bows on them. Likes to do it. Not any more. I could tell you a funny story about that girl and that off bay. Would make you laugh. Off horse is eight, near is ten, but might of been twin colts the way they work together. See? The teeth. Sound all over. Deep lungs. Feet fair and clean. How much? Ten dollars? For both? And the wagon – Oh, Jesus Christ! I'd shoot 'em for dog feed first. Oh, take 'em! Take 'em quick, mister. You're buying a little girl plaiting the forelocks, taking off her hair ribbons to make bows, standing back, head cocked, rubbing the soft noses with her cheek. You're buying years of work, toil in the sun; you're buying a sorrow that can't talk. But watch it mister. There's a premium goes with this pile of junk and the bay horses – so beautiful – a packet of bitterness to grow in your house and to flower, some day. We could have saved you, but you cut us down, and soon you will be cut down and there'll be none of us to save you.

And the tenant men came walking back, hands in their pockets, hats pulled down. Some bought a pint and drank it fast to make the impact hard and stunning. But they didn't laugh and they didn't dance. They didn't sing or pick the guitars. They walked back to the farms, hands in pockets and heads down, shoes kicking the red dust up.

Maybe we can start again, in the new rich land – in California, where the fruit grows. We'll start over.

But you can't start. Only a baby can start. You and me – why, we're all that's been. The anger of a moment, the thousand pictures, that's

us. This land, this red land, is us; and the flood years and the dust years and the drought years are us. We can't start again. The bitterness we sold to the junk man – he got it all right, but we have it still. And when the owner men told us to go, that's us; and when the tractor hit the house, that's us until we're dead. To California or any place – every one a drum-major leading a parade of hurts, marching with our bitterness. And some day – the armies of bitterness will all be going the same way. And they'll all walk together, and there'll be a dead terror from it.

The tenant men scuffed home to the farms through the red dust.

When everything that could be sold was sold, stoves and bedsteads, chairs and tables, little corner cupboards, tubs and tanks, still there were piles of possessions; and the women sat among them, turning them over and looking off beyond and back, pictures, square glasses, and here's a vase.

Now you know well what we can take and what we can't take. We'll be camping out – a few pots to cook and wash in, and mattresses and comforts, lanterns and buckets, and a piece of canvas. Use that for a tent. This kerosene can. Know what that is? That's the stove. And clothes – take all the clothes. And – the rifle? Wouldn't go out naked of a rifle. When shoes and clothes and food, when even hope is gone, we'll have the rifle. When Grampa came – did I tell you? – he had pepper and salt and a rifle. Nothing else. That goes. And a bottle for water. That just about fills us. Right up the sides of the trailer, and the kids can set in the trailer, and Granma on a mattress. Tools, a shovel and saw and wrench and pliers. An axe, too. We had that axe forty years. Look how she's wore down. And ropes, of course. The rest? Leave it – or burn it up.

And the children came.

If Mary takes that doll, that dirty rag doll, I got to take my Injun bow. I got to. An' this roun' stick – big as me. I might need this stick. I had this stick so long – a month, or maybe a year. I got to take it. And what's it like in California?

The women sat among the doomed things, turning them over and looking past them and back. This book. My father had it. He liked a book. *Pilgrim's Progress.* Used to read it. Got his name in it. And his pipe – still smells rank. And this picture – an angel. I looked at that before the fust three come – didn't seem to do much good. Think we could get this china dog in? Aunt Sadie brought it from the St Louis Fair. See? Wrote right on it. No, I guess not. Here's a letter my brother wrote the day before he died. Here's an old-time hat. These feathers – never got to use them. No, there isn't room.

How can we live without our lives? How will we know it's us without our past? No. Leave it. Burn it.

They sat and looked at it and burned it into their memories. How'll it be not to know what land's outside the door? How if you wake up in the night and know – and *know* the willow tree's not there? Can you live without the willow tree? Well, no, you can't. The willow tree is you. The pain on that mattress there – that dreadful pain – that's you.

And the children – if Sam takes his Injun bow an' his long roun' stick, I got to take two things. I choose the fluffy pilla. That's mine.

Suddenly they were nervous. Got to get out quick now. Can't wait. We can't wait. And they piled up the goods in the yards and set fire to them. They stood and watched them burning, and then frantically they loaded up the cars and drove away, drove in the dust. The dust hung in the air for a long time after the loaded cars had passed.

**John Steinbeck**

# Low Ground

Before the lid was on
The babe cried for his mush.
Before the child could walk
An egg hatched in the bush.

A Norseman got his ground
He put his plough in.
Before the corn was up
He built a house of stone.

Before the corn was cut
The sweat stung his eye.
After the sun set
A wolf took the boy.

Before the house was high
He dug a channel of sod.
Before the water ran
His thin wife was dead.

Before the ice gripped
His hay reached the roof.
When the holly berried
He made a song of his grief.

Before the drifts thawed
He tore the sedge from the bog,
His herd grazed on the common,
His hedge grew on the rigg.

He met a girl in the dale,
A rook cawed in the ash.
Before her belly swelled
The banks were all awash.

He carried bread to the field,
His bride baked the loaf.
When the gales came
A babe dropped with the leaf.

He made his tools anew,
The frost creaked in the wall.
She wove a year's clothes,
The snow reached the sill.

The days began to grow,
The cow calved in the hay.
The buds began to green,
The man began to die.

She took the seed to the field,
The babe lay by the dyke.
Before the corn was sown
Her heart began to break.

Before the shoots were up
He turned his face to the wall.
Before his feet were cold
His wife began to howl.

She gave milk to the calf,
She brewed ale for the feast,
She pulled the cow to the door
She gave the babe her breast.

Before her cheek sank,
The boy could hold a plough.
Before her hair was white
The fields began to grow.

Before her eyes were closed
His *ranes stretched a mile.
Before his shoulders bowed,
He got a wife in the dale.

**David Craig**

*Ranes were the terraces
on which the strips of the
open-field system were
sited on the steep sides of
the Yorkshire dales.

# Search for an Ancestor

I grew up in a little town called Henning, Tennessee, about fifty
miles west of Memphis, and I lived there in the home of my
grandmother, my mother's mother. Every summer my grandmother
would have visitors come to our home. They would be older
women of the family, her nieces, aunts and cousins, and every single
evening that I can remember, they would sit out on the front porch
in rocking-chairs, and I would sit behind my grandmother's
rocking-chair and listen to them talking. They would tell about
things that had happened to the family when they had been slaves,
and they went back and back and back. The furthest-back person
they would ever talk about was someone they described as 'the
African', and they would tell how this African had been brought on
ship to a place they pronounced as 'Napalis'. They told how he had
been bought off that ship by a man whose name was John Waller,
who had a plantation in a place called Spotsylvania County,
Virginia, and they told how the African had kept trying to escape.
The first three times he escaped he was caught, brought back, given
a worse beating each time, and then, the fourth time he escaped, he
had the misfortune to be caught by a professional slave-catcher. I
have since done some peripheral research on the profession of slave

catching and I think there's never been a more bestial one in the United States. This particular man brought the African back, and it was decided on the spot that he would be given a punishment at the decision of the slave-catcher. I grew up hearing how the slave was offered the punishment either of being castrated or of having a foot cut off with an axe against a tree stump. It was a very hideous act and it turned out it was to play a major role in keeping the African's story alive in a black family. In the middle of the 1700s, slaves, particularly male slaves, were sold back and forth so frequently that there was very little sense of family continuity among them. In that part of Virginia they were sold at auction and, on the average, each would bring around eight dollars. At the end of every slave auction there would be what they called a 'scrap sale'; slaves who were ill, otherwise incapacitated, would bring in smaller amounts, generally one dollar or less. When this particular slave managed to survive and then to convalesce, he posed an economic question to his master: slavery, after all, was an economic matter. Although he was crippled and hobbled around, he could do limited work around the house and yard-area of the plantation, so the master decided he would be worth more kept to do this limited work than he would be just sold away for less than one dollar in cash. And so he was kept on one plantation for what turned out to be quite a long period of time.

On that plantation, this slave met and mated with another slave. My grandmother and the others said that she was named Belle, the Big House cook, and of that union was born a little girl, who was given the name Kissy. When Kissy got to be four or five, and could begin to understand things, this African, whenever he got the chance, would take her by the hand (he knew her to be his daughter, she knew him to be her father – an unusual thing in slavery at that point) and lead her round the plantation. He would point out to her various natural objects and tell her the names for them in his native tongue: some sounds for *tree, rock, cow*. In the slave-cabin area, he would point out a banjo or a guitar and he would say one syllable, *ko*, and in time the little girl came to associate the sound *ko* with a banjo or a guitar. On the outer edges of the plantation there was a small river, and when they were out in that area, he would say to her something like *Kamby-Bolongo*, and this little girl came to know that this sound meant river.

All the Africans who were brought to the United States as slaves gradually learned a word here, a phrase there, of the new language, English. As this began to happen with this particular African, he would tell his daughter more involved things, little anecdotes about himself. He seemed to have a passion for trying to communicate to her a sense of his past. For instance, he would tell her how he had been captured. He told her he had not been far away from his village, chopping wood, when he had been set upon by four men, kidnapped, and taken into slavery. The first thing that happened to slaves when they got to a plantation was that they were given an Anglicized name: that was the first step in the psychic dehumanization of an individual – the removal from that individual of the name he had carried all his life, with which went, as it goes for us today, the sense of who we are. The master had given this African the name of 'Toby' but, whenever any of the other slaves used the word 'Toby', he would strenuously reject it and tell them his name was Kin-Tay.

Kissy stayed directly exposed to her father from Africa until she was sixteen years old. She had quite a considerable repertoire of knowledge about him, when she herself was sold away to a man named Tom Lea who had a much smaller plantation in North Carolina. It was on that plantation that Tom Lea became the father of Kissy's first child, a boy who was given the name of George. When George got to be about four or five, Kissy began to tell him the things she had learned from her father. Among the other slave children, his peers, he began to run into the common phenomenon that slave children rarely knew who their fathers were. He had something that made him singular: he had direct knowledge of a grandfather. The boy grew up and when he got into his teens, became a gamecock fighter: that was a great sport in the Ante-Bellum South. When he was about seventeen, he gained the nickname that he would take to his grave – 'Chicken George'.

When he was about eighteen, Chicken George took a mate, another slave, whose name was Matilda, and in time Matilda gave birth to seven children. On another plantation, a generation later, in another section of North Carolina, Chicken George would tell his children the story which had come down from his mother Kissy. Those children grew up, took mates and had children. One of them was named Tom. He became an apprentice blacksmith and was sold to a man named Murray who had a tobacco plantation in Alamance County, North Carolina. He met and mated with a slave whose name was Irene, the weaver of the plantation, and she bore him seven children. Tom the blacksmith would tell his seven children about something virtually unique among the slaves: direct knowledge of a great-great-grandfather. The youngest of his seven children was a little girl whose name was Cynthia, and Cynthia was to become my maternal grandmother. That was how it happened that I grew up in my grandmother's home in Tennessee, hearing from her that story which had passed down the family about all the rest of the family going back to that African who said his name was Kin-Tay, who called the river *Kamby-Bolongo*, and the guitar *ko*, and who said he had been chopping wood when he was captured. By the time I was in my mid-teens, I knew this story pretty well, having heard it for fully a decade.

I went to school briefly at small Black Land grant colleges around the South where my father was teaching, and when World War Two came along I went into the us Coastguards. It was the time when if you were black and you went into one of the Naval Services in the United States, you went into the Stewards' Department. You were mess-boy, you cleaned up the state rooms, waited on tables, washed the dishes, and, if you did well, advanced to cook. I became cook on a ship in the south-west Pacific during the war. It was boring. We would be put to sea for two or three months at a time before we could get ashore in Australia or New Zealand. My most precious possession was a portable typewriter. I had learned to type when I was in high school, and I would write letters to everybody I could think of: I would get thirty or forty letters at a time, simply because I wrote so much. Then I began trying to write marine dramas, sea stories. They didn't sell for a long time, but I kept writing for eight years, until finally a small magazine began to buy some of my stories. I stayed on in the Service, began to write for somewhat larger magazines, and finally, when I was thirty-seven, I retired from the Coastguards with twenty years service. At that time, something happened that seems to me to have been the first of a series of miracles that were to make it possible to pull together a document, a book of which I am now at the finishing stages, having to do in an unusual way with black history, black culture, black pride, relating to the whole area of blackness in Africa and the United States and the continuities.

The first thing that happened could scarcely have seemed to have less to do with blackness. *Playboy* asked me if I would fly over to London to do an interview with a film actress, Julie Christie. There were long gaps when I couldn't get to see her. One morning I was in the British Museum, and I came upon the Rosetta Stone. I had read how the French scholar, Champollion, had matched the unknown characters on the stone with the Greek, and had finally been able to prove that the demotic and the hieroglyphics had the same text as the Greek. That fascinated me: I would go around in London doing other things, but I would find my mind going back to that Rosetta Stone.

I was on a plane going back to the United States when an idea hit me. What Jean Champollion really did was to match the unknown with the known, and so find the meaning of what hitherto had been unknown. In that story always told in our family there had been a language: the sounds that this African always said when he pointed to different objects. Obviously, many sounds would have been lost in the transmission down the generations, but I could see that the sounds which had survived tended to be hard, angular sounds of the sort that would survive: like *ko*, Kin-Tay, *Kamby-Bolongo*. They had to be fragments of some native tongue. Could I possibly find out where these sounds had come from? My research assistant, George Simms, came up with a list of people who were very knowledgeable in the field of African linguistics. One of them was at the University of Wisconsin. His name was Doctor Jan Vansina. He had been trained in his native Belgium, and then at the

University of London's Oriental and African Studies department. He had worked in Africa, living in African villages, and had written a book called *The Oral Tradition*. In the Vansinas' living-room that evening, I told Dr Vansina everything I could remember from the time I was a little boy: every bit of the stories, the sounds, the names of the people, the chronology of the family. As an oral historian, he was particularly interested in the physical transmission of the story from one generation to another. The following morning, Dr Vansina came down with a very serious expression on his face. I learned that he had already been on the phone to knowledgeable colleagues of his. He said that they felt that the greatest possibility was that the sounds represented the Mandinka dialect. I had never heard of such a thing as Mandinka. From his knowledge of it, he began to guess-translate what those sounds had meant. There was a sound that probably meant the *beobab tree*, generic in West Africa: there was a sound that probably meant *cow*. I heard about something that could be said to look like a banjo, an instrument called the *kora*, well-known where Mandinka was spoken. Finally we came to *Kamby-Bolongo*: I heard that in Mandinka *bolongo* would mean *river* or *stream*. Preceded by *Kamby*, very probably it would mean *Gambia River*. I tend to be, if something hits me just right, very impulsive. It was Thursday morning when I heard the words *Gambia River*. On Monday morning I was in Africa.

On the Friday morning, I had looked among the names of African students in the United States. From that small country, the Gambia, the one I found who was physically closest to where I was was a fellow called Ebon Manga, attending Hamilton College at Clinton, New York. I hit that campus around 3.30, Friday afternoon, and practically snatched Ebon Manga out of an economics class. We got onto a Pan-American that night and flew to Dakar. From there we got a light plane and flew over to Yanda, near Bathurst. We took a van into Bathurst. Ebon and his father helped to assemble a group of about eight members of the Gambian Government, mature men who met me in the patio of the Hotel Atlantic in Bathurst. There I sat with them, telling them the stories that had been passed down. It gives me the quivers sometimes when I reflect how tissue-thin have been the hinges upon which this whole adventure has swung at one time or another. What these men in the Gambia reacted to most was a sound which I had no idea had any particular meaning. They said: 'There may be great significance in the fact that your forefather said his name was Kin-Tay. In our country, your older villages are often named from the families which founded those villages centuries ago.' And they showed me a little map, with names of villages like Kinte-Kundah Jenneh-Ya. They also told me about men of whom I had never heard called *griots*, who were like walking, living archives. A line of *griots* would know the history of one village, they told me, or of one large family clan. They told me that they would look about to see what *griot* might be able to help me.

I went back to the United States. About six weeks later, a letter came to me from the Gambia saying that when I was able it might be worthwhile for me to return – as casually as that. In about a week I was back in Bathurst. The same men with whom I had talked at the Atlantic Hotel told me that the word had been put out in the back-country, and a *griot* knowledgeable about the history of the Kinte clan had been found. 'Where is he?' I asked. I would have figured, from my experience as an American magazine writer, that the Government should have had him there with a public relations man for me to talk to. They said: 'He's in his village.' In order to see this man, I had to get together a total of fourteen people, three of which were interpreters, and four musicians – they told me that, in the back-country, the *griots* wouldn't talk without music in the background.

Mud walls, conical-roofed huts, thatched roofs: there were only about seventy people in the village. As soon as I saw a man, I knew somehow that he was the man we had come to see. Small of build with a pill-box hat and off-white robe: I was later to learn that his name was Kebba Kanga Fofana. The interpreter with me went straight to him. Meanwhile I had stepped into a succession of events that were almost traumatic in their emotional effect upon me. First, the people, about seventy of them, crowded very closely around me. I began to notice how they were staring at me. Their brows were forward and the intensity of the eyes was just raking. It was as if they wanted to know me in corpuscular detail: I dropped my eyes: I had this sensation of looking at my own hands, my own complexion, and I had a tremendous feeling within me, like a gale-force wind. I was looking at a crowd of people and, for the first time in my life, everybody in the crowd was jet-black in colour. That just hit me like a sledgehammer. And then, I had this second sledgehammer-type feeling: a kind of guilt, a feeling of being hybrid, of being impure among pure. Then the old man, Kebba Kanga Fofana, began to tell me, through the interpreters, the history of the Kinte clan.

*Griots* can talk for hours on end, telling the stories they have learned. Every now and then when the *griot* was spilling out lineage details of who married whom, who had what children and in what order, a couple of centuries ago, he would stop: a translation would come of some little detail about an individual – for example, that in the year of the Big Water he slew a water buffalo. Kebba Kanga Fofana said that the Kinte clan had begun in the country called Old Mali, and a branch of the clan had moved into Mauretania. In Old Mali, the clan had been characterized by the men being blacksmiths as a rule; the women were habitually potters and weavers. There had come out of Mauretania a son of the clan whose name was Kairaba Kunta Kinte. He came from Mauretania to the country of the Gambia. He stopped first in a village called Pakali N'Ding. He went next to a village called Jiffarong, and then to a village called

Juffure. It was in Juffure that he took his first wife, a Mandinka maiden whose name was Sireng. By her he begot two sons whose names were Janneh and Saloum. Then he took (Muslim men, plural marriages) a second wife. Her name was Yaisa, and by Yaisa he begot a son whose name was Omoro.

The three sons grew up in the village of Juffure, and when they came of age the older two, Janneh and Saloum, went away and founded a new village called to this day Kinte-Kundah Janneh-Ya. The youngest son, Omoro, stayed there until he had thirty-nine rains; and at the age of thirty rains he took a wife whose name was Binta Kebba. Between 1750 and 1760, there were born four sons to Omoro and Binta Kebba; Kunta, Lamin, Suwadu and Madi. When he named those four brothers, the old man stopped and the interpreter said: 'about the time the King's soldiers came'. That was one of the time-fixing references which *griots* use. Later, in London, I found the British Parliamentary records, because I had to know the date. He was talking about a group called Colonel O'Hare's Forces, which had been sent from London to the Gambia River to guard the then British-held fort, James Slave Fort, and the date was right on.

Then Kebba Kanga Fofana said: 'About the time the King's soldiers came, the eldest of these four sons, Kunta, went away from this village to chop wood, and he was never seen again.' I sat there with goose-pimples the size of lemons popping over me. He had no way of knowing that what he had told me meshed with what I had heard as a little boy on the front porch of my grandmother's home in Tennessee.

I suddenly became aware that the people of the village had formed a circle and were moving counter-clockwise around me. They were chanting: up, down, loud, soft. I had been sitting on a chair, and I popped up as if I had been full of helium. All I could do was stand up. Then there came the music that was always in the background. I remember my ears slowly becoming aware that I was hearing sounds I had to recognize from a *kora* player, who was singing. I was hearing in a way I could understand. I could distinguish the words 'Alex Haley'. I could understand Kinte. I didn't know then that, in the way of *griots*, my having come to that village, my having been found to be a descendant of that village, was there and then being recorded as part of the village's history. They carried me into the mosque, and there was a prayer. It was translated as: 'Praise be to Allah for one lost long from us whom God has returned.'

We finally had to go back. I had to return to America and, on the road going out, I was full of the emotion of it. We got to the first village, and I saw people lined up on either side of the road. The people in this village already knew what had happened in the village of Juffure. As we came close with the Land-Rover, the driver slowed down, and I was looking down at these people standing on

either side waving, a great cacophony of sound coming out of
them, from wizened elders to little naked youngsters. I thought it
was nothing but caprice: they were there, never having left Africa,
and I, symbolising to them all of us in America, happened to be
standing up in there simply because of the caprice – which of our
forefathers had been taken out. That was the only thing which had
made the difference. Then I gradually became aware what the sound
was they were crying out: 'Mr Kin-Tay, Mr Kin-Tay.' I'm a man,
but a sob rolled up from foot-level, and I just flung up my hands
and cried as I never had in my life. It seemed to me that if you
knew the story of how the black people in America had come there,
taken as slaves from all those countries, and you knew the
continuity of us as a people, then, whatever else you might do, you
really needed to start by weeping, because there were no words and
no actions which could ever assuage what had happened in that
terrible time in the history of both countries.

**Alex Haley**

NOBODY KNOWS ME.

WHO?

NOBODY SEES ME.

WHERE?

NOBODY LISTENS TO ME.

WHAT?

NOBODY CARES ABOUT ME.

YAWN

NOBODY TAKES ME SERIOUSLY.

HA HA HA HA HA HA HA HA

NOBODY NEEDS ME.

I NEED YOU.

I'M NOT READY.

©1973 JULES FEIFFER

# Mansie Considers Peedie Mary

Peedie Alice Mary is
My cousin, so we cannot kiss.
And yet I love my cousin fair:
She wears her seaboots with such an air.

**Ian Hamilton Finlay**

# Archives

```
generation upon
generation upon
generation upon
generation upon
generation upon
generation upon
generation upon
generation upon
generation upon
generation upon
generation upon
generation upon
generation upon
generation upon
generation upon
generation upon
generation upon
generation upon
generation upon
g neration upon
g neration up  n
g nerat on up  n
g nerat  n up  n
g nerat  n  p   n
g  erat  n  p   n
g  era   n  p   n
g  era   n      n
g  er    n      n
g  r     n      n
g        n      n
g        n
g
```

**Edwin Morgan**

# Acknowledgments

For permission to use copyright material acknowledgment is made to the following:

**Poems, Prose and Plays**

For 'Archives' from *Gnomes* by Edwin Morgan to the author and Akros Publications; for 'Song for Last Year's Wife' from *Little Johnny's Confession* by Brian Patten to the author and George Allen & Unwin (Publishers) Ltd; for 'Low Ground' by David Craig to the author; for extract from 'A Proper Marriage' by Doris Lessing to the author and Curtis Brown Ltd; for extract from 'A Very Easy Death' by Simone de Beauvoir, translated by Patrick O'Brian to the author, translator and Andre Deutsch Ltd; for 'Wife-Wooing' from *Pigeon Feathers and Other Stories* by John Updike to the author and Andre Deutsch Ltd; for 'The River-Merchant's Wife: A Letter' from *Collected Shorter Poems* by Ezra Pound to the author and Faber & Faber Ltd; for 'Roman Wall Blues' from *Collected Shorter Poems* by W. H. Auden to Faber & Faber Ltd; for 'Lizard' from *Histoires* by Jacques Prévert to the author and Editions Gallimard; for extract from 'Strange Meeting' by Susan Hill to the author and Hamish Hamilton Ltd; for 'Watching Song' from *Doors of Stone* by F. T. Prince to Rupert Hart-Davis Ltd/Granada Publishing Ltd; for 'Walter Llywach' from *Tares* by R. S. Thomas to the author and Rupert Hart-Davis Ltd/Granada Publishing Ltd; for extract from 'The Grapes of Wrath' by John Steinbeck to the author and William Heinemann Ltd; for 'Two Young Men, 23 to 24 Years Old' by C. P. Cavafy translated by Keeley and Sherrard to the translators and The Hogarth Press; for 'Tonight I Write Sadly' from *The Man Who Told His Love* by Pablo Neruda translated by Christopher Logue to the author, translator and Hope Leresche & Sayle; for extract from 'That's How It Was' by Maureen Duffy to the author and Hutchinson Publishing Group Ltd; for 'At the Draper's' from *Collected Poems of Thomas Hardy* by Thomas Hardy to The Trustees of the Hardy Estate and Macmillan London & Basingstoke; for 'Wedding Wind' from *The Less Deceived* by Philip Larkin to The Marvell Press; for 'Together We Are Building a Wall' by Sara O'Reilly to the author; for 'First Frost' from *Antiworlds* by Andrei Voznesensky translated by Stanley Kunitz to the author and Oxford University Press; for 'The Stone Boy' from *The Mistress and Other Stories* by Gina Berriault to the author and Laurence Pollinger Ltd; for 'Andromeda' by Connie Rosen to Harold Rosen; for 'Breaking the News' from *Children Are Civilians* by Heinrich Böll, translated by Leila Vennewitz to the author, translator and Secker & Warburg Ltd; for 'Hymeneal' by Janice Elliott to the author and Richard Scott Simon Ltd; for 'My Father in the Night Commanding No' from *At the End of the Open Road* by Louis Simpson to the author and Wesleyan University Press; for extract from 'Birth Without Violence' by F. Leboyer to the author and Wildwood House Ltd; for 'Norma' from *Mixed Doubles* by Alun Owen to the author and Felix de Wolfe & Associates.

Every effort has been made to trace owners of copyright material, but in some cases this has not proved possible. The publishers would be glad to hear from any further copyright owners of material reproduced in *Bonds*.

**Pictures** For the pictures on page 2 to Saul Steinberg; pages 8–9 Cornell Capa, Magnum, The John Hillelson Agency; pages 12–13 to The Imperial War Museum and Camera Press; page 15 to the Royal Academy of Art; pages 16–17 to Homer Sykes; page 18 to Geoff Howard; page 21 to The Munch Museum, Oslo; page 22 to Ria Eng; page 28 to Larry Herman; pages 30–31 to Judy Moraes; pages 32, 37 to Pierre-Marie Goulet; page 35 to Frederic Leboyer; page 38 to Cornell Capa, Magnum, The John Hillelson Agency; page 42 to Ronald Sheridan; page 43 to the Boston Museum of Fine Arts; page 45 to the Victoria and Albert Museum; page 46 to W. Eglon Shaw, the Sutcliffe Gallery; page 47 to the Basle Art Museum; page 55 to Janine Wiedel; pages 56–7 Jean Cocteau and Dover Publishing Inc.; page 59 to the Southampton Art Gallery; page 60 to the Museum of Modern Art, New York; page 61 to Ben Shahn and Cory, Adams and Mackay; pages 60–61 to Pablo Picasso; page 67 to Chris Schwarz; pages 68–9 Smith College Museum of Art, Massachusetts; page 71 to the Art Gallery of New South Wales; page 81 to Charles Harbutt, Magnum, The John Hillelson Agency; page 83 to Niklaus Walter; page 84 to the Tate Gallery; pages 90–91 to Allen Jones, Waddington and Tooth Galleries; pages 92–3 to Ronald Sheridan; page 95 to the Werner Forman Archive; page 99 to the Rijksmuseum, Amsterdam; page 100 to Colin Curwood; page 103 to the US Signal Corps; pages 105, 106–7, 109 to The Farm Security Administration, The Library of Congress, Washington; pages 110–11 to Fay Godwin; page 119 to Alex Haley and The Observer; page 120 to Jules Feiffer; page 121 to Camera Press; page 122 to Peter Smajic and the Gallery of Primitive Art Zagreb.

# List of Illustrations

# Index